D0801285

THE UPPER ROOM

YOUR PLACE TO MEET GOD

Sarah Wilke
Publisher

Lynne M. Deming
World Editor

INTERDENOMINATIONAL
INTERNATIONAL
INTERRACIAL

79 EDITIONS
37 LANGUAGES

The Upper Room
September–December 2012
Edited by Susan Hibbins

The Upper Room © BRF 2012
The Bible Reading Fellowship
15 The Chambers, Vineyard, Abingdon OX14 3FE
Tel: 01865 319700; Fax: 01865 319701
Email: enquiries@brf.org.uk
Website: www.brf.org.uk
BRF is a Registered Charity

ISBN 978 1 84101 846 1

Acknowledgments

The New Revised Standard Version of the Bible, Anglicized Edition, copyright © 1989, 1995 by the Division of Christian Education of the National Council of the Churches of Christ in the USA. Used by permission. All rights reserved.

The Holy Bible, New International Version, copyright © 1973, 1978, 1984 by International Bible Society. Used by permission of Hodder & Stoughton Publishers, a member of the Hachette Livre UK Group. All rights reserved. 'NIV' is a registered trademark of International Bible Society. UK trademark number 1448790.

Extracts from the Authorised Version of the Bible (The King James Bible), the rights in which are vested in the Crown, are reproduced by permission of the Crown's Patentee, Cambridge University Press.

Scriptures quoted from the Good News Bible published by The Bible Societies/HarperCollins Publishers Ltd, UK © American Bible Society 1966, 1971, 1976, 1992, used by permission.

Printed in the UK by HSW Print.

The Upper Room: how to use this book

The Upper Room is ideal in helping us spend a quiet time with God each day. Each daily entry is based on a passage of scripture, and is followed by a meditation and prayer. Each person who contributes a meditation to the magazine seeks to relate their experience of God in a way that will help those who use The Upper Room every day.

Here are some guidelines to help you make best use of The Upper Room:

1. Read the passage of Scripture. It is a good idea to read it more than once, in order to have a fuller understanding of what it is about and what you can learn from it.
2. Read the meditation. How does it relate to your own experience? Can you identify with what the writer has outlined from their own experience or understanding?
3. Pray the written prayer. Think about how you can use it to relate to people you know, or situations that need your prayers today.
4. Think about the contributor who has written the meditation. Some Upper Room users include this person in their prayers for the day.
5. Meditate on the 'Thought for the Day', the 'Link2Life' and the 'Prayer Focus', perhaps using them again as the focus for prayer or direction for action.

Why is it important to have a daily quiet time? Many people will agree that it is the best way of keeping in touch every day with the God who sustains us, and who sends us out to do his will and show his love to the people we encounter each day. Meeting with God in this way reassures us of his presence with us, helps us to discern his will for us and makes us part of his worldwide family of Christian people through our prayers.

I hope that you will be encouraged as you use the magazine regularly as part of your daily devotions, and that God will richly bless you as you read his word and seek to learn more about him.

Susan Hibbins
UK Editor

In Times of/For Help with . . .

Below is a list of entries in this copy of *The Upper Room* relating to situations or emotions with which we may need help:

Addiction: Dec 23, 31

Advent/Christmas: Dec 2, 4, 6, 7, 14, 15, 20, 23, 24, 25

Anger: Sept 5

Anxiety: Oct 19

Assurance: Nov 20

Bible reading: Sept 16, 17, 19; Oct 1, 8, 28, 30; Nov 8, 26; Dec 22, 27

Celebration: Dec 2, 11, 24

Change: Oct 22, 27, 30; Nov 24; Dec 20

Christian community: Sept 5; Oct 7

Compassion: Oct 31; Dec 23

Creation: Sept 1; Oct 31; Dec 3, 27, 30

Death/grief: Oct 6, 20, 30; Dec 2, 10

Evangelism: Sept 15, 16, 23; Oct 3

Failure: Sept 8; Oct 17; Nov 13; Dec 23

Family: Sept 7, 10, 28, 29; Oct 6, 19, 30; Nov 1, 12; Dec 24

Fear: Sept 18, 22; Oct 9, 12, 15, 19, 26

Financial concerns: Sept 17; Oct 2

Forgiveness: Sept 10, 28; Oct 5, 7; Nov 5, 19, 23; Dec 5, 14

Freedom: Dec 31

Friendship: Sept 15, 26; Oct 29; Nov 5

Giving: Oct 2, 18; Dec 4, 10, 13, 16, 26

God's goodness/love: Sept 9, 14, 24, 30; Nov 10, 17, 20; Dec 1, 16

God's power: Oct 27

God's presence: Sept 6, 15, 18, 22; Oct 14, 26; Nov 10; Dec 1, 6

God's provision: Sept 16; Nov 22; Dec 4, 19, 20

God's will: Sept 2, 9, 12, 13, 15; Oct 23

Growth: Sept 24, 29; Oct 1, 8, 10, 22, 27

Guidance: Sept 1, 25, 30; Oct 16; Dec 3

Hope/future: Sept 9, 14; Oct 14; Dec 7

Hospitality: Sept 23; Oct 5, 11

Healing/illness: Sept 4, 5, 18; Oct 6, 9, 27; Nov 1, 13, 15, 28; Dec 29

Job concerns: Oct 15, 24; Nov 7, 15, 22

Judging: Nov 2, 12, 25

Living our faith: Sept 5, 7, 11, 29, 30; Oct 8, 25; Nov 1, 3, 5, 30; Dec 26, 28

Loneliness: Oct 30; Dec 2

Loss: Sept 11, 25; Oct 30; Nov 7, 24

Materialism: Oct 2, 20; Dec 4, 19, 26

Mental illness: Nov 13

Mission: Sept 7, 23; Nov 2, 15; Dec 4

New beginnings: Dec 30

Obedience: Sept 1, 3, 7, 21; Oct 14, 25; Nov 11, 16, 29; Dec 15

Parenting: Sept 22, 26; Oct 1, 12, 26, 31; Nov 1, 6, 21; Dec 1, 11, 22, 25

Patience: Nov 14, 17

Peace/unrest: Oct 26; Nov 7, 28

Prayer: Sept 12; Oct 6, 19, 29; Nov 28; Dec 12, 29

Renewal: Sept 29

Repentance: Sept 29; Oct 17

Salvation: Oct 3; Nov 2; Dec 13, 17, 18

Security: Nov 24, 26

Serving: Sept 5, 21, 23, 26, 28, 29; Oct 8, 25; Nov 11, 14; Dec 23, 25, 26

Speaking about faith: Sept 4, 16, 28; Oct 6, 17, 21; Nov 1, 3, 23; Dec 17

Social issues: Oct 23, 31; Nov 15; Dec 10

Spiritual gifts: Dec 8, 18

Spiritual practices: Sept 27, 29; Oct 1, 4, 7; Nov 3, 8, 11, 24; Dec 5, 9, 17

Stewardship: Sept 2, 8, 26; Oct 2, 6, 18, 24; Nov 11, 22; Dec 4, 8, 10, 26

Strength: Nov 13

Tolerance: Oct 31; Nov 12, 25

Tragedy: Nov 1

Trust: Sept 22, 30; Oct 12; Nov 6; Dec 1

Connections

'If then there is any encouragement in Christ, any consolation from love, any sharing in the Spirit, any compassion and sympathy, make my joy complete: be of the same mind, having the same love, being in full accord and of one mind' (Philippians 2:1–2, NRSV).

Bernie Rodriques wanted to throw a going-away party. For two weeks, the South African grandmother had hosted two young American women in her home while they volunteered at the ministry that Bernie serves. But not enough of Bernie's colleagues could come to make it a proper party, so she reached out to her neighbours.

'You've seen these young women come and go each day,' she told them. 'Please help me give them a good send-off.'

One new neighbour was delighted by the invitation and brought her husband, children and a lovingly prepared dish to share. Many others also came, filled with good cheer and laden with homemade food.

It was a grand celebration, but Bernie was so focused on her hosting duties that she didn't make time for her *Upper Room* devotional until late evening. When she finally opened the 'little book' to the day's date, her eyes widened as she read the headline: 'Know Your Neighbours'. The devotion's writer, John M. Drescher of Pennsylvania, described how he had made a conscious effort to reach out to his new neighbours. Bernie couldn't help but think, 'That's just what I've done. This was meant for me.'

Bernie, who is also an Upper Room volunteer, shared her story with me in Johannesburg at the second of our Upper Room 'family reunion' gatherings around the world. Though her story is among the most moving I've heard, I've grown accustomed to readers telling me how often individual devotions speak to their own lives, how often reader and writer are 'of one mind' though they may live a continent apart. Paul counsels that this is as it should be. As Christians, the things we have in common do outnumber our differences.

I pray that you will make similar connections as you experience the stories in this edition of *The Upper Room*.

Sarah Wilke, Publisher

The Editor writes...

About a year ago I attended a course to learn to become a guide at Peterborough Cathedral. It was a fascinating ten weeks: we explored the cathedral from top to bottom, literally, creeping through a low passage beneath the present building, which had once been part of the Saxon abbey on the same site; and scaling the total of 180 spiral steps that led from ground level up to the massive roof beams and beyond, to the roof itself.

As well as the history of the building, we heard of all the different people who had had the vision, at different times, to begin to build, or to carry on work that others had started. Cathedrals take centuries to complete, and the people who began to build them, who saw the cornerstones laid and toiled for years to raise the first areas of today's building in the 1100s, never saw the work completed. Craftsmen, who had talents for carving stone or wood, for working in stained glass, for manoeuvring large blocks of masonry so that they stayed upright and in place—all such people gave of their best during the time they worked there, even though the finished building lay far in the future.

Our service for God's kingdom is similar, whether it is as part of our church community's work, or our day-to-day discipleship. We may feel that what we are trying to do is a very small part of God's work. The projects we are engaged in at church may take a long time to come to fruition and may not show much success to begin with. The way in which we try to live day by day, and our efforts to try to help people may all seem a contribution that makes little difference to the progress of God's work in the world. Yet final results lie with God. Our task is to contribute, to do our best, and to trust that God will take what we do and use it in the best way for the furthering of his kingdom.

Susan Hibbins
Editor of the UK edition

P.S. The Bible readings are selected with great care, and we urge you to include the suggested reading in your devotional time.

The Narrow Path

Read Proverbs 4:20–27

'Stand at the crossroads, and look, and ask for the ancient paths, where the good way lies; and walk in it.'
Jeremiah 6:16 (NRSV)

I live in a village at one side of the beautiful River Clyde. Since I was a child, I have been amazed by the narrowing of the river at low tide. When the sandbanks and mudflats become a magnet for birds, it seems perfectly feasible that we should be able to walk or swim across to the other side.

However, this appearance is deceptive because the river has a deadly deep, narrow channel that allows ships to pass between Glasgow and the Lower Clyde. Only the captains of those vessels know exactly where to steer in order to stay afloat, because of strategically placed buoys.

We can be taken in by appearances and activities that seem like a good idea but actually take us into danger. Life is often as deceptive as that river. We are easily deceived when we rely on our own judgment. Only God can see the bigger picture and steer us in the safest direction. The channel is marked out for us by the wisdom of the Bible. The way becomes clear to us as we pray and walk daily with God. How reassuring that God knows the way. The question is, are we willing to listen and to follow God's guidance?

Prayer: *Dear God, guide and inspiration of humanity, thank you that you love us enough to direct us. Forgive us when we think we know best. Keep our minds and hearts ever focused on you. Amen*

Thought for the day: God is the Captain, and we are the crew.

Rosemary Gemmell (Langbank, Scotland)

PRAYER FOCUS: THOSE WHO WORK AT SEA

Special

Read Zechariah 14:20–21

[God] has made everything suitable for its time.
Ecclesiastes 3:11 (NRSV)

'Special' read the large sign taped to the side of a bus. Students on a summer mission trip named the bus 'Special' after the mission team purchased it for the church in La Paz, Honduras, where they had worked many summers. As their team leader I can assure you the bus is aptly named. Special has a cracked windscreen that cannot be repaired because a replacement is difficult, if not impossible to find in Honduras. Sometimes Special develops other problems that have to be attended to. Nevertheless, every week the bus winds up and down the dirt mountain roads to bring to church people who otherwise would not be able to attend.

But really, anything dedicated for use in serving God, becomes special. Today's scripture reading from Zechariah speaks of the holiness of even the cups and cooking pots in the temple. Because they were used for God's purposes they were holy. If cups and pots can be special to the Lord, then so can an old bus with a cracked windscreen.

God's people are a bit like that, too. Living for God's purposes makes us holy, and we are all special in our own ways. God created each of us different, for a unique purpose.

Prayer: *Dear heavenly Father, help us to find and embrace your purpose for life. Teach us how to appreciate the specialness in ourselves and others. In Jesus' name. Amen*

Thought for the day: Giving ourselves to God makes us holy.

Harriet Michael (Kentucky, US)

PRAYER FOCUS: THE PEOPLE OF HONDURAS

Firm Foundation

Read Matthew 7:24–27

The rain fell, the floods came, and the winds blew and beat on that house, but it did not fall, because it had been founded on rock.
Matthew 7:24–25 (NRSV)

From my second-floor flat, I can see construction underway on another block of flats across the street. I had never seen a construction project in progress before, so I have watched carefully.

What drew my attention was that the soil the construction workers were removing was muddy and unstable. Dry soil was brought in from another location, and several layers were spread across the plot until the ground was firm. At that point the workers excavated, leaving an enormous hollow for the foundation of the building.

This was all part of creating a firm foundation. I thought, how many times do we disregard what God wants for each of us? How many times have we followed our own ideas without building on God's teachings? The psalmist said, 'Unless the Lord builds the house, those who build it labour in vain' (Psalm 127:1), and Jesus reminds us of that truth in today's reading.

I want to build my life on that sure foundation.

Prayer: *Dear God, rock of our life, redirect our steps when we stray from the path that you want us to follow. Give us the wisdom to realise when we are going the wrong way and to call on you for direction. Amen*

Thought for the day: Following God's teachings is a firm foundation for life.

Carlos Evelio Montoya (Cali, Colombia)

I am Blessed

Read Jeremiah 17:5–8
Blessed are those who trust in the Lord, whose trust is the Lord.
Jeremiah 17:7 (NRSV)

While in Houston for my grandson's radiation treatment for cancer, I took an early morning walk. Hurrying to get back before the humid August air became unbearable, I noticed another person walking at a much faster pace. I slowed to let him pass and offered a customary 'Hi.' I don't usually begin a conversation while exercising, but this particular morning I added, 'How are you doing today?' He turned to look without slowing his pace; and with an immense smile he answered with conviction, 'I'm blessed.'

Continuing my walk, I pondered his words. As a child of God with everlasting hope and forgiveness, I too am blessed. Dealing with a difficult situation, such as a loved one's cancer treatments, we're apt to forget that we are indeed blessed. We forget to trust God no matter what our circumstances are, and to be thankful for doctors, nurses, caring friends and families. An unknown man reminded me that I am blessed and that my family is blessed. I doubt I will ever meet him again in this life, but his confident words are etched deeply and echo repeatedly in my thoughts: I am blessed.

Prayer: *Dear God, thank you for eternal hope through Jesus Christ and for the blessings that come from knowing you. Amen*

Thought for the day: God reminds us often that we are blessed.

Beverly Taylor (Colorado, US)

PRAYER FOCUS: CANCER RESEARCHERS

Meet a Need

Read Titus 3:1–15

Let people learn to devote themselves to good works in order to meet urgent needs, so that they may not be unproductive.
Titus 3:14 (NRSV)

A few years ago, a group of my wife's friends and I had a garage sale. We sold clothing, appliances and items that had been gathering dust in our loft. By the end of the sale, we had collected more than one hundred dollars. We donated the money to a friend who had met with an accident at work and was recovering in a hospital's intensive care unit.

For Christians, doing such acts should not be remarkable. Scripture gives special emphasis to Christians' engaging in good deeds. Much of the letter to Titus is devoted to instructions on godly living, urging believers to be ready, to be an example and to be zealous in doing good deeds. In fact, the letter mentions good works five times. Only three chapters long, its final instruction is, 'Let people learn to devote themselves to good works.'

How can we apply that scripture teaching today? Titus 3:14 tells us to meet pressing needs. Does someone you know have an urgent need? Perhaps a family member or friend needs financial assistance, or a colleague is hurting and needs someone to listen. Each of us can meet needs today and every day.

Prayer: *Dear Lord, teach us to be responsive to the needs of other people. Amen*

Thought for the day: Every day is a good day to serve in Christ's name.

Marc Villa-Real (Philippines)

A Matter of Focus

Read Matthew 14:22–33

Let us fix our eyes on Jesus, the author and perfecter of our faith, who for the joy set before him endured the cross, scorning its shame, and sat down at the right hand of the throne of God.
Hebrews 12:2 (NIV)

After deciding to learn to ride a motorcycle, I took a training course offered at our nearby community college. The instructors stressed the importance of focusing on the road ahead, scanning for potential hazards and planning how to deal with them. We were instructed not to look immediately in front of the motorcycle or to the side but to look ahead, especially on curves, so that we would not fall off or leave the road.

The Bible gives us similar instruction. Today's reading from Matthew 14 is one example. Peter initially followed the practice my instructors suggested. He knew where he wanted to be when he stepped out of the boat. Peter was focused on Jesus. However, the storm around him caused him to lose that focus, and he started to sink. That's when Jesus reached out to Peter and brought him to safety.

We too may have difficulty focusing on Jesus when we encounter problems and overwhelming situations. Health problems, financial difficulties or relationships that have gone awry can distract us as the wind and the waves affected Peter. But when we remember to focus on where we want to be—with Christ—he will reach out to us and bring us safely back into his presence.

Prayer: *Dear God, sustainer of life, help us to keep our eyes, our minds and our hearts focused on you at all times and in every situation. Amen*

Thought for the day: When we follow Christ's example, we live wisely.

Carol Forehand (Iowa, US)

A Christ Carrier

Read 1 Peter 2:9–12
Whatever you do, in word or deed, do everything in the name of the Lord Jesus, giving thanks to God the Father through him.
Colossians 3:17 (NRSV)

While studying our family's genealogy, a distant cousin of mine discovered that some relatives on my mother's side were from eastern Germany. In the 1700s, these ancestors fled religious persecution in Germany to seek freedom in America. Their German name, Christophel, means 'Christ carrier', and in one of his letters my cousin exclaimed, 'We have a rich Christian heritage.'

But that is not unique. 'Surrounded by so great a cloud of witnesses', as Hebrews 12:1 says, all believers have a rich Christian heritage. Each of us in our own way is meant to be a 'Christ carrier'. We all carry Christ because we bear his name and because God's Spirit dwells in us.

In a much more visible way, we present Christ to the world through our words, attitudes and actions, reflecting the Lord's message to the world. Our mission field may be as close as speaking to a neighbour across the fence, or it may be in some faraway country. But we can all carry Christ's name and message to those around us.

Prayer: *Dear Father, thank you for those who came before us, proclaiming the truth of life in Christ. Help us to reflect to others the love you have for them and to tell them about you. Amen*

Thought for the day: Today I will carry Christ wherever I go.

Paula Geister (Michigan, US)

Steward or Owner?

Read Genesis 2:15–17

Love the Lord your God with all your heart and with all your soul and with all your mind… And the second is like it: Love your neighbour as yourself.

Matthew 22:37, 39 (NIV)

For generations we humans have been blaming Adam and Eve for our woes, ignoring the truth that we disobey God just as they did. True, Adam and Eve ate from the forbidden tree, but the Bible doesn't tell us that they did further harm.

On our part, however, instead of carrying God's love and mercy to other creatures, we kill, destroy and endanger without thinking about what we are doing. We have turned God-given freedom into absolute power, using the world as if it is our own, not God's world in which we live as stewards.

We do this in large and small ways. For example, when my mother died, our family went to our ancestral town for 14 days of funeral celebrations, as is our custom. To do this, my father left his home in the hands of a caretaker. My father is responsible for a distant relative, a nine-year-old boy. On our return, not one of my father's twelve full-grown egg-laying chickens was to be found. When asked, the caretaker said, 'I used them to feed your nephew.'

Like the caretaker, we use up rather than care for God's creation. We make excuses, claiming that we can do so because God wants us to live well, but often behind our choices are greed and selfishness.

Prayer: *Dear God, help us to honour the work you have given us, to care for Earth rather than destroy it. In Jesus' name. Amen*

Thought for the day: Do I behave as if I am an owner or a caretaker of God's garden?

Joshua Kyeremeh (Hovedstaden, Denmark)

Steadfast Love

Read Psalm 6

O Lord, do not rebuke me in your anger, or discipline me in your wrath. Be gracious to me, O Lord, for I am languishing… O Lord—how long? Turn, O Lord, save my life; deliver me for the sake of your steadfast love.
Psalm 6:1–4 (NRSV)

The first thought of many people when they have a serious illness is: what did I do wrong? Why is God punishing me? I don't know why this is so ingrained in us. But most of us have said it or wondered it at least once.

David is no exception. However, God does not punish us by sending illness or calamity, though this is what we often feel. I and others from our church who visit people in hospital try to correct this false understanding whenever we encounter it. After all, what kind of God would that be? Not the kind of God we know through Jesus! But since it's such a common reaction, maybe we sometimes need to express the feeling so we can clear it away and move on to the truth of God's unwavering love and care, the truth of God's desire for good and health and wholeness for each of us.

David's question, 'How long?' is really a statement of faith. For while the duration of our struggle may be uncertain, the reality of God's presence is never in doubt. As Psalm 6:4 says, God's love for us is never in doubt; it is 'steadfast'.

Prayer: *Dear God, help us in times of struggle to remember that your love for each of us is steadfast. Amen*

Thought for the day: Even when we doubt God, he is present with us.

Link2Life: *Visit someone who is housebound through illness.*

Dan G. Johnson (Florida, US)

When it Hurts

Read Romans 12:14–21

God's love has been poured into our hearts through the Holy Spirit that has been given to us.

Romans 5:5 (NRSV)

When I recently read the above verse, I was reminded of an incident that happened early in my marriage. One of our relatives said something very negative about me, and I was deeply hurt. When my husband came home that night, he vowed never to speak to this relative again.

Nevertheless, within a week we were able to visit them. Although it was a little awkward at first, we soon forgot about the incident and later even helped them in a time of need. At that time, I thought I was able to forgive and avoid holding a grudge because of my light-hearted nature. And because I'm a Christian, I attributed it to God.

Over the years since then I have taken an active role in attending and leading Bible studies. Studying scripture has helped me to realise it was only because of 'God's love poured into our hearts' that I was able to forgive and love those who hurt me so much. I know that even when we are hurt deeply and long for revenge, we can commit our feelings to God, who can turn our hurt into love. With God's love in us, we in turn are able to love those who hurt us.

Prayer: *Loving God, thank you for your love that fills our hearts. Help those struggling to forgive others who have hurt them. In Jesus' name we pray. Amen*

Thought for the day: God's love is greater than any hurt we will encounter.

Lata Samuel (Bangalore, India)

Remembering 9/11

Read Joel 2:23–27

The spirit of the Lord [has] anointed me… to provide for those who mourn in Zion—to give them a garland instead of ashes, the oil of gladness instead of mourning, the mantle of praise instead of a faint spirit.

Isaiah 61:1, 3 (NRSV)

Last year marked the 10th anniversary of the attack on the World Trade Center towers in New York City. For me, one of the most poignant images displayed during the remembrances was the picture of doctors and nurses at Manhattan hospitals waiting for patients who never came. The number of people treated was fewer than expected because many of the people who were trapped in the two buildings were simply turned into dust.

Even after horrible tragedies, our attention quickly turns back to the mundane—the squabbling of politicians, hostility among opposed groups, the petty pressures that obscure our deeper, larger, higher calling as people created by God. But still I couldn't forget that image of the waiting hospital workers.

Where do we go after loss, disappointment, tragedy? God is always at work to create new life, abundant life, eternal life from the dust of our own and others' lives. What is the new work that God wants us to help bring out of the dust of others' losses? Each one of us 'dusty' people is called to become God's agent, working to bring fullness of life in a dusty, wounded world.

Prayer: *Dear God, our creator, we are only dust, but you make wonderful creations from dust. Help us to see and to do our part in bringing new life to our homes, our neighbourhoods and your world. Amen*

Thought for the day: Where can I be part of God's work of bringing new life?

James A. Harnish (Florida, US)

Constant Conversation

Read 1 Thessalonians 5:16–24
Pray without ceasing.
1 Thessalonians 5:17 (KJV)

After many years of doubt and denial, I was determined to rediscover my faith. But getting back into the habit of praying was the hardest part. Then I noticed that in quiet moments during the day, the verse 'Pray without ceasing' would pop into my head. I felt confused and guilty. If I can't even remember to pray before I eat, I thought, how can I remember to pray all the time?

One day while out picking blueberries, I realised that I was 'talking' to God—not a formal prayer, but more like talking to a friend about how thankful I was for the sweet berries. I caught myself doing the same thing at other times such as when I was washing dishes or driving—simple conversations about what happened to be on my mind. I am also taking more time to listen. In these 'conversations', God's 'voice' comes through as feelings moving in my heart, or thoughts flowing through my mind. Sometimes I hear God speak to me through words from a friend. When this happens God is working through both of us and we both benefit from his wisdom.

I still struggle, but the relationship I am developing with God by learning how to 'pray without ceasing' sustains me.

Prayer: *Dear Lord, keep us in constant conversation with you. Amen*

Thought for the day: Whenever we breathe a thought to God, we are praying.

Hope Rouse-Lurie (Alabama, US)

PRAYER FOCUS: THOSE TRYING TO REKINDLE THEIR FAITH

An Unfailing Guide

Read Exodus 13:17–22

Jesus said, 'I am the light of the world. Whoever follows me will never walk in darkness but will have the light of life.'
John 8:12 (NRSV)

The night was dark; clouds obscured the moon and stars. I was on my tractor ploughing the field before a coming rainstorm made the soil too wet to till. The area I still had to plough was shaped irregularly. The tractor's lights illuminated only a short space ahead of me and a narrow strip on each side. I followed the perimeter of the field in ever-narrowing circles. The tractor lights enabled me to follow my previous circuit, but soon I lost all sense of direction. I had no idea which way I was going.

Then I looked up. Three miles away, I could see the four red lights of a radio-broadcasting tower. I knew that direction was south. As long as I could keep those lights in mind, I would know where I was; I should never get lost.

Sometimes I become similarly disoriented in life. I rush around, busily involved in making a living, raising a family, serving in my church and community and countless other tasks. These good and necessary parts of life can close us in so that we see only our small circle, as with me on my tractor. Just as looking to the radio tower restored my sense of direction in the field, I can look to Christ Jesus to restore direction in my daily life.

Prayer: *Dear gracious God, thank you for Jesus Christ, our light and our guide. Help us to follow that light. Amen*

Thought for the day: How does my life reflect Christ's light to those around me?

Lloyd Kitching (Manitoba, Canada)

Day by Day

Read John 15:1–11

[God] is able to accomplish abundantly far more than all we can ask or imagine.

Ephesians 3:20 (NRSV)

The telephone call was a bombshell. A sombre voice informed me that cancer cells had invaded my bones. After moments of frightened reflection, I thought to pray, remembering the words of Jesus, 'Ask, and it will be given you' (Matthew 7:7). As I wondered how to pray, the words 'Abide in me as I abide in you' (John 15:4) also came to mind.

We do not have to plead with God. We can always come into God's presence with thanksgiving and hear his wonderful words of love, 'Do not be afraid, for I am your God; I will strengthen you, I will help you' (Isaiah 41:10). God may not give exactly what we ask, but he will respond in love. The mystery and greatness of God are beyond our comprehension. Each day is his gift, with the best yet to come.

Whether we have one day or ten years of life ahead with family and friends, God's love will sustain us and bless us. Working in us, God 'is able to accomplish abundantly far more than all we can ask or imagine' (Ephesians 3:20). I remind myself of this truth day by day.

Prayer: *Dear holy God, take our every moment of pain and bless it with your love. In the name of Jesus we pray. Amen*

Thought for the day: God hears every earnest prayer.

Warren G. Spellman (Nebraska, US)

Near to Us

Read Genesis 28:11–21
Jacob woke from his sleep and said, ' Surely the Lord is in this place—and I did not know it!'
Genesis 28:16 (NRSV)

From a young age I was apprehensive and restless, searching for something to fill a void within me and give meaning to my existence. At 19 I travelled to England to study English and to continue my spiritual search in a faraway land, another environment, separated from my family. There I went to work and lived an independent life, continuing to seek answers to my questions.

One day I met a missionary family on the bus. They invited me to their home for a meeting with other international students. I accepted, thinking it a good opportunity to meet other people and practise my English. I came to know this family as kind and full of peace, joy and much love. They read and taught the Bible. I got closer to them because I wanted to know what they had that I didn't. I soon learned what it was and that it was what I had been searching for. They had Jesus in their hearts. I had only religion; what I wanted was relationship.

I thank God for bringing this family into my life. Through them I found the reason for my existence. I returned to Colombia to a new life of purpose, joyful that I had finally discovered a God who had been very close to me all along.

Prayer: *Dear God of all peoples, help us teach those near us about you so they do not have to travel to other lands to learn the truth. Amen*

Thought for the day: Within each of us is a space that only God can fill.

Link2Life: *Consider financially supporting a mission family.*
Yaneth Orozco Zapata (Cali, Colombia)

No Excuses Please!

Read 2 Timothy 3:14–17

'Do not fear, for I am with you; do not be dismayed, for I am your God. I will strengthen you and help you.'
Isaiah 41:10 (NIV)

When I lost my job some years ago, I found a new position in another area of the country, in the town where my mother-in-law lived. While my family prepared to move, I stayed with her. Our family had not been attending church for several years, and I knew we needed to go back. My mother-in-law taught an adult Bible class and assumed that I would go to church. So I did.

I attended a different Bible class and felt comfortable joining in the discussions and learning about God's word. One day the teacher told me, 'The class has talked about it, and you are leading next week.' As I recited excuses not to do it, she left the leader's guide on the table and walked out. I picked up the guide and went home. By Tuesday evening I was sure I could not lead the class, and I told my mother-in-law. She said, 'OK, you take a few minutes to tell that to God. And then next Sunday, tell the class.' Knowing neither of those was an option, I started to pray, asking God for guidance and help.

As the week went by, the words from Isaiah 41:10 kept ringing in my head. When Sunday came, I was ready to talk about what I felt God had shown me in relation to the day's scripture reading. I learned from this experience that God empowers us to do what he calls us to do. And by the way, I'm now a lay leader in the church—and my family is back in church, too.

Prayer: *Steadfast and loving God, you are always ready to help us. Slow us down so we can listen to you, thank you and praise you. Amen*

Thought for the day: Being with God's people helps us to know and to do his will.

Carl (Bud) Whipple (Tennessee, US)

Newfound Strength

Read Psalm 42:1–8

As the deer pants for streams of water, so my soul pants for you, O God.
Psalm 42:1 (NIV)

One day a woman entered my office with a copy of *The Upper Room*. She was from a neighbouring area of the country and had come to our city to seek a new job. Her family was in a financial crisis. On top of this, two of her children had died in a freak accident at sea. As her family was going through this loss, a friend had given her a copy of *The Upper Room*.

The Upper Room had served as a great source of blessing for her because she could relate to others who had suffered difficult times. *The Upper Room* became the first thing she reached for every morning; it gave her the courage to face another day.

Her story touched me. Many times I have postponed reading *The Upper Room* or the Bible because I was too busy. This woman read *The Upper Room* with great devotion and came to share her experience with me because she had seen my picture on the cover of the magazine. I learned from her that though we may be comfortable in every way, we still thirst for the love of Christ, just as the deer pants for water.

Prayer: *Dear Lord Jesus, we thank you for the gift of your word. Help those who are deprived of necessities to experience your love. Amen*

Thought for the day: Only the living water can satisfy our soul's thirst.

Leena Vijaykumar (Bangalore, India)

PRAYER FOCUS: THOSE WHO EDIT *THE UPPER ROOM*   23

Not Seeing, and Believing

Read John 9:1–7, 35–38

'Who is he, sir?' the man asked. 'Tell me so that I may believe in him.'
John 9:36 (NIV)

I was told that I would lie on my back during the cataract surgery and look into the bright light from the microscope being used in the operation to remove the cataract from my eye. As I lay waiting for the surgery to begin, someone said, 'Doctor Smith is in the room.' A few seconds later, my surgery began.

It occurred to me later that I had not seen the man who restored my sight. But I believed that he was in the room and ready to help restore my vision.

Like me on the day of my surgery, the blind man whose story is told in the ninth chapter of John's Gospel, did not see Jesus before he was healed. Jesus sent him to the Pool of Siloam to wash the mud from his eyes. Later when Jesus saw the man and asked, 'Do you believe in the Son of Man?' the man gave an honest answer: 'Who is he, sir? Tell me so that I may believe in him.' Jesus said, 'You have now seen him; in fact, he is the one speaking with you.' Then the man said, 'Lord, I believe.'

In many ways, ways that are meaningful to us personally, Christ comes to each of us individually. Even when we cannot see him clearly or do not know who he is, Christ reminds us that he is the Son of God, and that he has been with us all along.

Prayer: *Dear Lord, open our eyes to see you this day. In Jesus Christ. Amen*

Thought for the day: Christ is with us to help us even when we're unaware of it.

Terry Lee Davis (Florida, US)

Believer-come-Lately

Read Psalm 146

[The prodigal's father said,] 'This son of mine was dead and is alive again; he was lost and is found!'
Luke 15:24 (NRSV)

Reading Psalm 146, I discovered that each line from this psalm spoke to me. I am now 62 years old, and I came to God three years ago. My faith didn't come suddenly, as some experience it. But I made a commitment to a long-term Bible study course. In the beginning of that course, all of it was quite boring for me; I forced myself to read and study the Bible. I was close to giving up. But God heard my knock and opened the door (see Matthew 7:7). Suddenly, I noticed that nature is wonderful and people can be amiable. I began to ponder the basic values of life, and I yearned to study more.

Everything completely changed once I decided to try to live as a Christian. I was no longer going back to my old life; I was walking on a familiar road towards home. Outwardly my life was as it had been before, but inwardly it all felt totally new for me.

Today I am a second-year student at theological college. Moreover, I now realise how much time I have lost in my life. Yes, I already have one higher-education degree from my youth that has helped me to come through my life. But I have started thinking more about the spiritual aspect of life now. I feel as if I have woken up from sleep. Thanks be to God!

Prayer: *Dear God, you are powerful! You lift us out of the darkness with your mighty hand, and we are very grateful. Thank you. Amen*

Thought for the day: It is never too late to answer God's call.

Link2Life: *For information on studies such as Valdeko was involved in, go to www.upperroom.org*

Valdeko Dreifeld (Voru Maakond, Estonia)

A Truth Revealed

Read Acts 3:1–16

'Why do you wonder at this, or why do you stare at us, as though by our own power or piety we had made [this man] walk?'
Acts 3:12 (NRSV)

As long as I can remember my mother had a gold watch. When I inherited it I cherished it, wound it every day and was delighted that it kept perfect time.

After I had had it for about a year, it stopped. I took it to the watchmaker and expressed my hope that it only needed cleaning. 'Perhaps,' came the reply, 'it needs a new battery.' And it did.

For over a hundred days, I had wound my watch and believed that it had been kept going by my power. But its good operation was due to the power inside it. I thought about the things I try to do for the Lord. How easy it is to believe that any good works we do are our own achievements when, in truth, it is the Holy Spirit within us that makes them possible.

I hope I will always remember that our ability to serve our Lord is because of his power within me.

Prayer: *Dear Lord, may we always be aware of your Holy Spirit enabling us to serve you in helping those around us. Amen*

Thought for the day: Our power to serve comes not from ourselves, but from the Spirit.

Janet Wood (Canterbury, England)

Intelligent Influence

Read Mark 10:13–16

I tell you the truth, anyone who will not receive the kingdom of God like a little child will never enter it.
Mark 10:15 (NIV)

I recently developed a theory called 'Intelligent Influence'.™ In the context of Christianity, this simply means that in order to live the life that God calls us to live, we have consciously to manage how we are influenced and how we influence others. We all have power to influence others.

Recently my 21-month-old daughter demonstrated her influence at dinner one night. As we sat down to eat, Ashley grabbed our hands and bowed her head. My wife and I were astonished that our daughter had carefully watched us pray before every meal and was influenced to do the same.

This simple act by a young child convinced me of the importance of being aware of the influence we all have. Furthermore, as Christians we are called to allow God to guide our prayer life and every other part of our lives as well. We can also strive to demonstrate and be a positive Christian influence in the lives of others by attempting to do what God calls us to do, minute by minute, wherever we find ourselves.

Prayer: *Dear God, teach us to receive the kingdom of God like a child, paying attention to you and those around us. Help us influence others to worship you every minute of every day. Amen*

Thought for the day: Allowing God to influence us will transform our lives.

Dale G. Caldwell (New Jersey, US)

PRAYER FOCUS: THOSE IGNORING GOD'S INFLUENCE

Watched Over

Read Psalm 121
Truly the eye of the Lord is on those who fear him, on those who hope in his steadfast love.
Psalm 33:18 (NRSV)

On a summer afternoon our family went to the beach. Our two small daughters were enjoying the sand and sea. They played for quite a while, oblivious to the growing mass of people setting up beach umbrellas all around them.

When the girls decided to return to us, they could not tell exactly where they were. But we were watching them. They looked disoriented, momentarily paralysed. Their father quickly set out to get them. They were never in danger and never out of our sight.

As children of God, we may frequently find ourselves feeling lost and disoriented. In a sea of confusion, how good it is to know that God is vigilant and nearby! He knows how we feel and what we are facing. And God, our protector, loves us and watches over us.

Prayer: *Dear loving God, without your guidance and kindness we would be lost in the world. As Jesus taught us, we pray, 'Our Father in heaven, hallowed be your name, your kingdom come, your will be done on earth as it is in heaven. Give us today our daily bread. Forgive us our debts, as we also have forgiven our debtors. And lead us not into temptation, but deliver us from the evil one.'* Amen*

Thought for the day: Those who trust in God are never alone.

Mabel M. de Varas (Arica, Chile)

A Divine Appointment

Read Matthew 25:31–40

Jesus said, 'I was hungry and you fed me, thirsty and you gave me a drink.'
Matthew 25:35 (GNB)

One cold day as my husband and I were travelling, we stopped for petrol. As we pulled into a garage, a stranger approached us. Cautiously, I lowered my car window. Unsure as to how we could help, I asked the man what he needed.

As it turned out, my husband and I were able to provide not only physical food to a homeless man but also the spiritual food that comes in knowing Jesus Christ. I became excited by the opportunity that stood before us, knowing that this was a divine appointment. God trusted us to obey the Bible's words about providing food to the hungry (Matthew 25:31–46) and entertaining strangers (Hebrews 13:2).

This experience helped us to remember that God gives to us so we can give to others. We could easily have kept the food we had packed for ourselves. But we discovered a need to be met, and we gave freely.

The scripture reading tells us that when we meet others' needs, we are doing these things for the Lord.

Prayer: *Dear Lord, teach us to recognise the opportunities you bring us to serve you by serving others. Amen*

Thought for the day: Gratitude for what we have can displace worry about what we may lack.

Renee McCoy (Mississippi, US)

Christ-like Character

Read Galatians 5:22–26

The fruit of the spirit is love, joy, peace, patience, kindness, generosity, faithfulness, gentleness and self-control.
Galatians 5:22–23 (NRSV)

For many years I thought I was a relatively good Christian. I participated in several ministries and served others in my profession as a physician. I was a leader in my church as well. But one day the Holy Spirit reminded me of Jesus' stern warning to some people who apparently did many good works: 'I never knew you; go away from me' (Matthew 7:23). Why would Jesus say this?

As I searched for an answer, the Holy Spirit reminded me that what matters most with God is not so much what we do as who we are. Paul tells us that God has set us apart from the beginning 'to become like his son' (Romans 8:29, GNB), the first among many of God's children. God's children: that's who we are, not what we do. Yes, we are called to bear the fruit of joy, peace, patience, kindness, generosity, faithfulness, gentleness and self-control—but the list in Galatians begins with love. Becoming like Christ is the foundation for developing the other virtues and living out God's love in our actions.

When we commit ourselves to allow the Holy Spirit to shape Christ-like character in us, we can be assured that at the end of our lives we will be welcomed. We will hear our Lord say, 'Come, you that are blessed by my Father, inherit the kingdom prepared for you from the foundation of the world' (Matthew 25:34).

Prayer: *Dear loving God, help us to open our hearts to the love you offer us so that we may become true brothers and sisters of Christ, in whose name we pray. Amen*

Thought for the day: We live well when we follow Christ in self-giving love.

Gunawan Kosasih (Jakarta, Indonesia)

A Strong Arm

Read Isaiah 41:8–13

If I take the wings of the morning and settle at the farthest limits of the sea, even there your hand shall lead me, and your right hand shall hold me fast.
Psalm 139:9–10 (NRSV)

When I lost my sight, I learned sighted-guide techniques, in which the blind person holds a sighted person's arm just above the elbow and follows them. Later I received training with guide dogs. The blind person holds the dog's harness handle with the left hand, which leaves the right hand free to open doors, carry a purse or bag, or hold a child's hand. In recent years, I have not had a dog guide. I often use sighted-guide assistance from my husband, friends and family members. Having become accustomed to holding a guide dog's harness with my left hand, I prefer to hold my guide's right arm. It seems the most natural and comfortable way to travel.

One day during my scripture reading, I noticed a reference to God's 'strong right arm'. For me, this image of God as my guide in life, alongside me to keep me safe and secure, brought me comfort. This reference to God's strong right arm spoke to my need for reassurance. I began to find similar references again and again as I read the Bible. I thank God for being with me in all circumstances, guiding my way. I know that I can depend on him to lead me with love and care.

Prayer: *Dear God, you are present in every season of life to offer guidance, strength and comfort. We praise and thank you that we are never left alone. Amen*

Thought for the day: How do I experience God guiding me?

Karen E. Brown (Mississippi, US)

On My Doorstep

Read Romans 12:9–13

We are to use our different gifts in accordance with the grace God has given us… Whoever shares with others should do it generously.
Romans 12:6, 8 (GNB)

After I had had two children in two years, I couldn't be counted on to attend church—mostly because, often, one or both of my children would have the sniffles. Ironically, before this time, I was on the church staff in children's ministry, where daily I could use my gift of teaching. I mourned the loss of my ministry.

One morning a friend, who is also a stay-at-home mum, phoned me in tears, overwhelmed and lonely. I told her I would go to her house and bring my children to play with hers. We talked all morning about our similar struggles and she seemed to grow stronger.

Later I thought of another childhood friend. She is a mother of six, on benefits, with no car and utterly alone with no support from her family. Though I continually feel inadequate in the face of her needs, I'm beginning to see various ways I can help. I am learning through my relationships with these women that being a friend can be a powerful, challenging ministry.

Prayer: *Dear God, our companion, help us to see that you always have ways to use us, no matter what our circumstances are. Show us how we can serve. Amen*

Thought for the day: We can serve God where we are, wherever we are.

Link2Life: *Reach out to a young parent who may be feeling overwhelmed.*

Renee Lannan (Pennsylvania, US)

Letting Go

Read Philippians 4: 5b–7

I can do everything through him who gives me strength.
Philippians 4:13 (NIV)

It was still dark when I woke. My mind immediately clicked into gear, labouring up life's steep hill of problems. Wheels of thought were turning but getting nowhere fast. What was I to do about my disabled son's plans to move away from all he knew? How was I, his carer, going to make him understand the drastic consequences of such a decision? My head throbbed. I sighed, pulled back the bed-clothes and made my way downstairs.

Coffee mug in hand, I stared at an open magazine on the kitchen table. It depicted a child releasing balloons. Her hand was open, her upturned face a picture of pure delight. I realised then that I needed to let go of my problems and put them into God's capable hands. I couldn't hold on to my problems and hold his hand at the same time. I needed to let him take control. With God in the driver's seat Problems Hill wouldn't appear quite so steep.

Prayer: *Lord God, thank you for showing me that in order to hold your hand I need to let go of everything else: all my worry and fear. I can do nothing in my own strength. From this day let us journey together, hand-in-hand. Amen*

Thought for the day: With God, no problem is too big.

Julia Cutting (East Yorkshire, England)

Golden Apples

Read Matthew 18:15–35

A word fitly spoken is like apples of gold in a setting of silver.
Proverbs 25:11 (NRSV)

Away from home for a conference, I found myself in a noisy restaurant with two of my colleagues. A hockey game blared from six televisions around the room. Dishes clattered, and everyone cheered when the home team scored. I felt overwhelmed by my chaotic surroundings. To make matters worse, one colleague wouldn't stop talking. As soon as we sat down, she began to recount years of conflict with her mother-in-law. Her tirade ended with the declaration, 'I will never speak to her again!'

I wondered if I should sympathise or keep quiet. Unexpectedly, our other colleague spoke up. She said gently, 'Could you ever forgive your mother-in-law?' Her question surprised me. The surroundings of competitive sports, clinking glasses and sleek, corporate diners seemed to fade. Silence hung over the three of us. In a moment the conversation had turned from ordinary to holy.

How I admired my friend! In spite of our surroundings, she did not lose sight of who she was and what she believed. A barrage of words could not confuse her. With one question she invited us to consider something we all struggle with: forgiveness.

Prayer: *Forgive us, O God, for our reluctance to forgive others. Make us ever grateful for the way you have forgiven us, and help us to show your mercy to those who hurt us. Amen*

Thought for the day: A gentle response can transform tense moments.

Holly Dickson-Ramos (Ontario, Canada)

PRAYER FOCUS: SOMEONE I HAVE NOT FORGIVEN

Old Water

Read Isaiah 43:18–21

Thus says the Lord: 'Do not remember the former things, or consider the things of old. I am about to do a new thing.'

Isaiah 43:18–19 (NRSV)

My daughter scowled. 'Is this old water?' she asked. Before it was common to drink bottled water, we kept plastic water canteens in our car as we travelled the long distances between towns in West Texas and eastern New Mexico. However, when we did not replace the water for a while, what had once been refreshing began to taste like stale plastic. My daughter, wanting refreshment, refused to drink old water.

As with the old water in our canteens, many times we offer to our friends, fellow Christians and even ourselves the old work of God in our lives. Our relationship with God was fresh—once. But it can become stale. Yes, there might be enough power in it to save someone who is about to die of spiritual thirst. But our faith is not vibrant, refreshing living water.

When my relationship with God goes stale, it first shows inside me. I begin to refer to my experience with God in the past tense, and I feel discontent. Then the staleness shows in the way I interact with my family, friends and acquaintances. I am less at peace, less patient and more irritable. At these times I need to pray, read the Bible and ask the Holy Spirit to examine me for sin. My connection with God can become fresh again as I read a devotional book, serve others in Jesus' name and attend worship. My soul doesn't like old water either. No soul does.

Prayer: *Dear Lord, show us how to keep our relationship with you fresh.*

Thought for the day: Come to God daily for fresh faith to share with others.

Brad Reeves (Texas, US)

Lead or Follow?

Read Joshua 3:1–4

In all your ways acknowledge [the Lord], and he will make your paths straight.
Proverbs 3:6 (NIV)

Joe was a defiant, sullen boy who entered my classroom mid-year and challenged me at every turn. His life had been difficult, and he had been given very few choices in his short life. He was determined to control my actions and his circumstances, even though he had little understanding of where that might lead. But I held my ground firmly until he came to realise that I cared about him and had his best interests at heart. By the end of the year, he knew I loved him, and he trusted me to teach and guide him.

I have discovered that in my relationship with God I am often like Joe, trying to take control of my circumstances out of either fear or frustration. I run out ahead of God, like the men in our Bible reading for today. The ark represented the presence of God, and they were supposed to follow behind it, allowing it to lead them—especially since they had no idea where they were going.

As I learn to pray and to follow God's lead, I am learning not to rush ahead or try to take control. Rather, like Joe with me, I am coming to believe that God truly loves me and can be trusted to teach me and to guide me.

Prayer: *Dear Father, help us to realise that we can trust you. Teach us to wait and pray rather than rush ahead into situations that might hold danger for us or others. Amen*

Thought for the day: Following God can help us avoid a lot of wrong turns.

Valerie Bryant-Bennett (Tennessee, US)

Seek the Lord

Read Psalm 119:97–104
You shall love the Lord your God with all your heart, and with all your soul, and with all your mind, and with all your strength.
Mark 12:30 (NRSV)

When my son, Yutaka, was nine months old, he began to hold on to the sofa to walk. One day, I had left my Bible on the sofa and was playing with my son. He saw the Bible and walked toward it. I brought him back several times to the corner of the sofa, but he became frantic, fervently seeking out the Bible. I brought him back so many times that I eventually let him touch the Bible. My son, with an exceptionally big smile, touched the cover and then joyfully covered his head with the Bible.

When I saw him do this, I thought of Mark 12:30 and was deeply moved. I realised that the posture of Christians who yearn for God, love him and want to learn his word should be like my son's. As the Bible was for Yutaka, God is within our reach, and if we seek God, he will answer. Our steps may be uncertain; but as we steadily turn our hearts and eyes to God, giving our best, we come to know and love God.

Prayer: *Dear God, we thank you for being near to us. May we seek you and, throughout our lives, submit ourselves to you and love you. In Jesus' name, we pray. Amen*

Thought for the day: Choosing to seek God opens the door to a life of joy.

Hirono Shinomiya (Shizuoka Prefecture, Japan)

PRAYER FOCUS: WEARY PARENTS

What Pleases God

Read James 2:14–18
Faith by itself, if it is not accompanied by action, is dead.
James 2:17 (NIV)

We hear daily reports of weather destruction, death, wars and economic decline. We hear continual cries from churches and relief organisations to help those in need, both physically and financially. Sometimes I find myself withdrawing from these pleas. I reason that I am a widow, a senior citizen, and that I need to hold on to the little I have for my own use. But then I am reminded by God of a situation we faced a few years ago.

My husband was out of work for several months, and we were behind with our mortgage. We prayed for mercy and help. A few days later a couple knocked on our door and said, 'We feel that God wants us to give you this,' and handed us a cheque. The amount was enough to pay all our overdue mortgage payments. The couple didn't have much to live on either, yet they gave to us so that we would not lose our home. They listened to God's prompting, regardless of their own situation.

Even though we live in difficult times, I pray that we are willing to give what we can to help others. Help could be a monetary gift, driving a neighbour to a doctor's visit or making a meal for someone who is ill. Our willingness to help meet the needs of others and to respond in faith pleases God.

Prayer: *Dear Lord, help us always to be willing to share with others what you give us. Amen*

Thought for the day: Who is God prompting me to help today?

Carol S. Lewis (Illinois, US)

PRAYER FOCUS: THOSE IN DANGER OF LOSING THEIR HOME

The Moment of Salvation

Read John 3:1–21

Jesus answered [Nicodemus], 'I am telling you the truth: no one can see the Kingdom of God without being born again.'
John 3:3 (GNB)

Growing up, I sometimes found it discouraging that I couldn't remember an exact moment when I became a Christian. Then I feared that I couldn't remember it because I had actually never become a Christian at all. This worry would inspire me to commit my life again to Jesus in some sort of childlike, salvation-insurance prayer.

As a teenager I didn't have a dramatic testimony to give when I went to a Christian holiday camp. I often wasn't sure what to say when people asked when and how I became a Christian. When others would talk enthusiastically about a powerful, definitive time of conversion, I was left feeling as if my Christian faith wasn't as good as theirs—simply because I could not look back and identify a point when my Christian walk began.

With time, I have come to realise that my experience of being born again spiritually can be much like being born physically. I don't remember when I was born, but that doesn't mean that it didn't happen. Neither does the fact that I don't remember when I was born as a Christian mean that it didn't happen. The evidence of my natural birth can be seen in my life as I live, just as I hope the evidence of my life in Christ can be seen as I grow in my faith and seek to love, serve, honour and obey God in everything I do.

Prayer: *Dear loving God, thank you for the assurance we can have of our salvation in Christ Jesus. Amen*

Thought for the day: The evidence of new birth is a changed life.

Joanna Ronalds (Victoria, Australia)

Dirty Corners

Read Psalm 51: 6–7, 10

Wash away all my iniquity and cleanse me from my sin.
Psalm 51:2 (NIV)

The car stood bright and shiny in front of the garage, and looked almost new. It had been cleaned for us while we went and did our shopping at the supermarket. We were off to a family wedding in a few days' time, and I wanted it to look its best, so when we reached home, I emptied out all the items from the boot to make sure there was enough room for our luggage.

When I opened the doors I found areas and crevices that could not be cleaned at the garage because the car had been locked, yet showed up once the doors were opened wide. The corners were full of dirt that needed a small wet brush to get it out. Superficially the car had looked splendid, but deeper inspection showed hidden dirt that needed cleansing. It made me think of the dark, hidden crevices of my own life, that no one else knows about except God. I prayed there and then that God would do whatever it takes in my life to make me truly clean.

Prayer: *Heavenly Father, you know us through and through. You know the hidden places of our lives. Work your cleansing power in them today, we pray, in Jesus' name. Amen*

Thought for the day: Jesus came into the world that we might know cleansing and forgiveness.

Bernard Lelliott (Sussex, England)

Just a Prank

Read Galatians 6:7–10

Confess your sins to one to another, and pray one for another, so that you may be healed.
James 5:16 (NRSV)

Many years ago I drove to another city one rainy afternoon to see a baseball game. After the game was over, I drove through a large puddle in the car park and splashed a group of people. I did so intentionally, thinking it would be fun—just a prank. I heard one woman exclaim, 'My new dress!' Others in the group started to react angrily. I quickly drove away to escape their wrath.

I didn't enjoy the prank; I felt guilty then and afterwards. Although I have forgiveness in Christ for this and my other sins (see Ephesians 1:7), I still feel lingering regret and remorse when I recall that incident. If I could, I would write or telephone those people, apologise, ask their forgiveness and offer to make restitution, such as reimbursing them for the cost of dry cleaning their clothes. But I cannot do that. I don't know their names; I never even got a good look at their faces.

Nevertheless, there are some things I can do. I can seek, with God's help, to grow in Christ-like character. I can be kind and considerate toward others, and I can refrain from malicious or hurtful behaviour. And when someone else wrongs or inconveniences me, I can remember how much God has forgiven me.

Prayer: *Dear Lord Jesus, help us to love one another as you have loved us. In your name we pray. Amen*

Thought for the day: Real repentance leads to a changed heart and changed behaviour.

Robby Lucke (Florida, US)

Sighs too Deep for Words

Read Romans 8:18–27

The Spirit helps us in our weakness; for we do not know how to pray as we ought, but that very Spirit intercedes with sighs too deep for words.
Romans 8:26 (NRSV)

As I walked down the cold, sterile hospital hallway, I sensed that my family would ask me to pray. What would I say? Surely I could rely on my ministerial training? Yet I knew that this prayer would be unlike any I had prayed before.

When I rounded the corner to my grandfather's room in the intensive care unit, they were waiting. Their faces were weary with lack of sleep and moist with tears of grief over a difficult decision. This night would be my grandfather's last. When the time came to begin removing the tubes and drips, each of us grabbed the hand of the person next to us, and everyone looked at me. Suddenly all of my training seemed worthless. We stood in silence as I searched for the right words. I had none. I remembered Romans 8:26 and began praying its words aloud. Then in my mind I heard the beautiful opening theme of John Rutter's *Requiem*, and I prayed my way through its text: 'Grant [him] rest eternal, O God, and let perpetual light shine on [him].'

I am thankful that the merciful presence of God is not dependent on my knowledge and abilities. I am inadequate, but the Spirit helps me in my weakness. I am not called to bring comfort on my own or to show mercy on my own but rather to be a vessel through which God's love can touch us, by the power of the Holy Spirit. And that's the best any of us can be.

Prayer: *Dear loving God, whose mercy extends beyond the limits of human capacity, let us be vessels for your healing love. Amen*

Thought for the day: God's Spirit can equip us for each day's challenges.

Charlie Overton (Tennessee, US)

PRAYER FOCUS: THOSE FACING LIFE-AND-DEATH DECISIONS

Supper's Ready

Read 1 Corinthians 11:23–26

'Let anyone who is thirsty come to me and let the one who believes in me drink.'
John 7:37 (NRSV)

We were gathered for closing worship at a consultation on ministry in Russia. Mission supporters from churches across the United States and pastors and laity from churches across Eurasia filled the room. As Russian-speaking Christians listened to a translation through headsets, the local leader told us that there are three important phrases to learn in any language: 'I love you', 'I forgive you' and 'Supper's ready.' Then we prepared for Holy Communion.

The blessing was given, the bread was broken, the cup was lifted. After repeating three phrases to us—You are loved. You are forgiven. Supper is ready—the minister invited us to take Communion, saying, 'Come.' I moved to the front of the room and stood before two Russian women. They spoke to me in their language and served me. I don't know the exact translation of their words in that moment. But I heard the words of Christ in my heart, 'I love you. I forgive you. Supper's ready.' And I was fed.

Since then, each time I am served Holy Communion, I hear that I matter, that I am accepted, that I belong—and I am changed. I continue to be changed, strengthened to serve and to live so others will come to know themselves as loved by God and feel welcomed at his table as one of the family.

Prayer: *Dear holy God, what a joy it is to realise that all believers are bound together in your name! Strengthen us to serve and to love others into your family. Amen*

Thought for the day: You are loved. You are forgiven. Supper's ready. Come.

Joan Floyd (Tennessee, US)

The Garment of Life

Read Colossians 3:12–17

[You] have put on the new self, which is being renewed in knowledge in the image of its Creator.
Colossians 3:10 (NIV)

When my daughter was young, I made her clothes. My favourite part of that work was the preparation: selecting a pattern, the fabric and the colour, and finally the trim. I loved bringing the materials home and showing them to my daughter so that she could get an idea of what was in store. After the fun of shopping and previewing, the real work began. Dedicated time and skill turned a piece of cloth into something she could enjoy wearing. But until the work was done, the garment was no more than a nice intention.

It is much the same with what we learn from God's word. We can read the Bible, highlight favourite passages, and make notes in the margins. We can attend Bible study classes, hear sermons regularly and discuss what we've read. But actually doing something with God's word is the real work, the evidence that we have read and studied the words of scripture.

We determine to take God's instructions into our minds and hearts—and then to clothe ourselves in what we've learned. Only then does the word of God become embodied in us and make a difference in our lives and in the lives of those we encounter.

Prayer: *Dear Father, strengthen our resolve to live as your word teaches us. May we be doers of your word, not just hearers (see James 1:22). Amen*

Thought for the day: Once we hear God's word, the real work begins.

Pat Rowland (Tennessee, US)

Another Chance To Live

Read Psalm 34:1–10
The eyes of the Lord are on the righteous.
Psalm 34:15 (NRSV)

In the early morning of 14 July 2009, I was involved in a road accident. I was coming from the post office on a motorbike, when a vehicle hit me from behind. I heard a loud bang and was instantly filled with fear. The next thing I recall from that experience is lying in a hospital bed two days later.

My motorbike was damaged beyond repair, but I thank the Lord that I was not hurt more severely. When I regained consciousness, the doctor told me I had only a few fractures and minor injuries to my arms. God gave me another chance to live. It was by grace that I survived to see this day. Surely God's eyes are on us!

I have never felt such intense fear in my life as during that accident. I believed that I was about to die. I feel privileged that I was allowed a glimpse of God's greatness and that I was given another chance at life. I want to do more for God, to serve more. I'll hold on to my faith and hope.

Prayer: *Dear Lord God, hear our cry and deliver us out of all our troubles. Amen*

Thought for the day: Every day is another chance to live life more fully for God.

Dunford Ogolla (Nyanza, Kenya)

PRAYER FOCUS: THOSE RECOVERING AFTER ACCIDENTS

The Sprouting Seed

Read Matthew 13:1–8, 23

'Abide in me as I abide in you. Just as the branch cannot bear fruit by itself unless it abides in the vine, neither can you unless you abide in me.'
John 15:4 (NRSV)

I am a farmer; I grow corn and soybeans. Recently as I was examining my newly emerging plants, I felt that God was talking to me, teaching me a lesson from the sprouting seed. Once a seed is placed in the warm, moist soil, the first sprout is a small root that goes further down into the soil to absorb moisture and nutrients. This action prepares the seed to send a shoot up to receive sunlight as it begins the long process of making food for further plant growth. Eventually, the plant will grow and spread over the soil.

Like the soybean and corn sprouts sending the roots into the soil, a Christian's action is to delve into God's word, the Bible, in order to grow spiritually and to produce fruit. The fruit grows when we spread the Good News and lead people to Christ. We can do this by telling our story—what God has done for us. Sometimes we use words; but always we can tell our story by living so that others can see Christ in us.

Just as emerging plants receive the sunlight, we want to receive what God sends our way to strengthen us and encourage us for whatever lies ahead. When we do this, God can use us to produce fruit for the kingdom's sake.

Prayer: *Dear God, fountain of life, help us to grow in faith and love through reading, studying and obeying your word. Amen*

Thought for the day: God helps us to grow so that we can produce spiritual fruit.

Link2Life: *Visit a farm and talk to a farmer about how the crops grow.*
James H. McKelvey (Tennessee, US)

True Hospitality

Read Luke 14:7–14

When you give a banquet, invite the poor, the crippled, the lame and the blind. And you will be blessed, because they cannot repay you.
Luke 14:13–14 (NRSV)

In my work as a minister, I often visited people in nursing homes who were suffering from some form of dementia. I knew that within an hour or so of my leaving, many of them had forgotten who I was or even that I had visited at all. I sometimes reasoned that unless a nursing home employee or family member saw me, I would receive no credit for my ministry to that person.

This passage in Luke says otherwise. Jesus warns us that true hospitality has nothing to do with receiving a reward for our actions. True hospitality is giving without the hope of being paid back. True hospitality grows out of our love for God and our desire to be Christ in the world, not out of a desire to build or protect our ego or public image.

I might have felt that my visits to dementia patients were lost ministry moments; but in truth they may have been the more perfect ministry of my life.

Prayer: *Dear God, show us how we can create nurturing and holy ground today. Free us from self-interest and help us to serve for your glory. In Christ's name we pray. Amen*

Thought for the day: Every good deed done for Christ counts eternally.

Link2Life: *Visit a local nursing home and spend time with a resident who does not have regular visitors.*

Anna Shirey (Missouri, US)

Giant Crabs

Read Mark 4:35–41

Do not let your hearts be troubled and do not be afraid.
John 14:27 (NIV)

When I was seven, my father took me fishing on a remote beach. As I was too young to fish, I was content to sit in my small beach chair and play with my toys. When my father had gone into the water to make a cast, I noticed a crab that had quietly emerged from a hole not far from me. More menacing than its poised claw were the creature's black eyes, which appeared to be fixed on me. Soon, I noticed another crab, and another, until a legion of giant crabs seemed to be preparing to descend upon me. Out of fright, I cried out, 'Dad! Dad!'

Hearing my cry, my dad looked at me with concern, reeled in his line and began to walk back toward me. As my father drew near, the host of crabs scurried back into their holes. When I recounted to my father the story of the crabs, he smiled. He knew that fear was unnecessary, that the crabs would not hurt me; but for the rest of the day, my dad did not leave me alone to fend for myself against the crabs.

Most of our fears may seem unwarranted to God. But like my dad who understood and stayed close to me, God nevertheless does not leave us alone.

Prayer: *Dear God, when we are afraid, give us faith, courage and trust. Help us to remember that you are always with us. Amen*

Thought for the day: God never leaves us alone to fend for ourselves.

Ishai Nickels (Virginia, US)

Stay the Course

Read James 1:2–8

Blessed is anyone who endures temptation. Such a one has stood the test and will receive the crown of life that the Lord has promised to those who love him.
James 1:12 (NRSV)

One of my favourite weekend pastimes is riding my bicycle on a lane near my home. The lane is actually an old two-lane highway that was abandoned when a four-lane bypass was constructed nearby. Cyclists, joggers, skaters and people on horseback can now enjoy the old road without fear of meeting traffic.

The old road, for the most part smoothly paved and easy to ride, has some potholes. Sometimes I inadvertently run into them when I'm not paying attention. When that happens, I try harder to focus on where I'm riding.

So it is with my faith. When my life seems to be going smoothly, faith is effortless. But when trouble or temptation comes near, I find it more difficult to stay the course. That's when I try harder to focus on my faith to get me through the hard times.

I have never finished a bike ride and thought 'I wish I hadn't done that.' Instead, I always feel a sense of accomplishment and satisfaction, especially when the ride has been difficult. Likewise, we can become stronger as we face life's challenges even when our situation seems overwhelming.

Prayer: *Dear Lord, guide us along our faith journey when we stumble on obstacles along the way. Help us to always stay focused on our faith. Amen*

Thought for the day: Exercising our faith builds spiritual muscle.

Janet M. Kerns (Virginia, US)

Suffering in the Life of a Christian

Read 2 Corinthians 4:16–18

Our light and momentary troubles are achieving for us an eternal glory that far outweighs them all.
2 Corinthians 4:17 (NIV)

'Where was God on 9/11?' many asked. The fact is that God's children are in the world and share the sufferings of the world. On 9/11 God was with every one of those victims, granting them hope beyond the circumstances of that moment. God does not cause such tragedies, but he is present in them.

'[God] does not willingly afflict or grieve anyone' (Lamentations 3:33, NRSV). When famine, cot deaths, robberies, muggings, shootings and the like happen, it is not because God has forsaken us. The psalmist declared, '[The Lord's] kingdom rules over all' (Psalm 103:19). When awful things happen, God in no sense causes them or takes delight in our misery. But God does work through them to draw us into closer relationship.

God gave us free will and with it the freedom to choose wrongly in our decisions. But we can also make good choices: 'Everyone who calls on the name of the Lord will be saved' (Acts 2:21, Romans 10:13). One day soon God will close the curtain on evil and with it all suffering and sorrow. Then we shall see the final end to the Christian faith, 'Christ in [us], the hope of glory' (Colossians 1:27).

Prayer: *Dear God, we know that, as humans, we cannot avoid suffering, but that when we suffer we can always rely on you for comfort and hope. Amen*

Thought for the day: After [we] have suffered for a little while… God… will… restore, support, strengthen and establish us (1 Peter 5:10, NRSV).

Jim Brunner (Arizona, US)

The Lord is Near

Read Psalm 27

The Lord is close to the brokenhearted and saves those who are crushed in spirit.
Psalm 34:18 (NIV)

Despite the warning signs of other staff members losing their jobs and work slowing down, I was unprepared for the meeting with senior managers who told me that I was to be made redundant. I was stunned. I had worked for 15 years in Christian publishing, in a job where I thought God wanted me to be.

Three months later, my mother died after a long period of failing health. She and I had been very close. While I was glad that her struggles were at an end, I felt overwhelmed with sadness and curiously afraid. Two of the main concerns that had filled my days—my work and caring for my mother—had suddenly come to a full stop. What was happening?

A kind friend sent me a card expressing her concern for me. Her message included the words from Psalm 34:18 quoted above. I felt as if a small light had been switched on at the end of the tunnel where I was walking. It may have been only a pinprick of light, but it was there. I kept that card near me; I read it every day. I felt reassured that however many blows we have to contend with in life, in all our circumstances the Lord is very near to us to bind up our wounds, to heal us and, in time, to restore us to fullness of life.

Prayer: *Dear God of compassion, when sorrows threaten to overwhelm us, remind us of your presence and help us to remember that you are always near. Amen*

Thought for the day: I will walk in confidence today because the Lord walks by my side.

Susan Hibbins (Lincolnshire, England)

PRAYER FOCUS: THE RECENTLY BEREAVED

Finding the Way

Read John 14:5–12

Jesus answered, 'I am the way and the truth and the life.'
John 14:6 (NIV)

Our family has enjoyed hiking throughout New England. Some of the paths are harder to follow than others—not just because of steep hills and treacherous drops but also because they are obscured in the woods. Sometimes we start on a well-marked path, only to find that the forest has overgrown it so that we are not sure which way to go.

Getting lost is a hiker's nightmare. At minimum, it can be a long detour; at worst, it can become a fight for survival. Getting lost is far less likely on a clear path system. A good system is well mapped and marked, often using a 'blaze system' to show which way to go. A blaze is a paint patch painted along the path: hikers who follow these won't get lost. A properly blazed path shows the way clearly even at the most complicated intersections.

I often think of the Bible as my map and Jesus as the blaze. God did not put us on this earth without guidance. God made sure—as a good guide does—that we have the supplies we need for the journey. When I am unsure of a step to take or a choice to make, I look to the Bible, review Jesus' life, and pray. Then, like a blaze on the path, Christ's example guides me along.

Prayer: *Dear God, thank you for sending your Son so that we can see your way more clearly. Help us to look for your path, and give us the courage and strength to follow it. Amen*

Thought for the day: Following Jesus' example makes our choices clearer.

Link2Life: *Help blaze a path for someone else on the journey. Invite a friend to church.*

Dawn M. Adams (Massachusetts, US)

The Apology

Read Ephesians 4:29–32

Let no evil talk come out of your mouths, but only what is useful for building up, as there is need, so that your words may give grace to those who hear.
Ephesians 4:29 (NRSV)

Thoughtlessly, I had spoken harshly to a shop assistant. She hadn't done anything wrong; she was simply a convenient person on whom to vent my frustration. Once outside the shop, I realised how badly I had behaved. I remembered the times I had received similar treatment. Some customers seem to take assistants for granted, as nameless and faceless recipients for our anger and irritation. I felt ashamed; I realised that I had just done that to another.

After a few moments I went back inside and apologised for my behaviour. The assistant's face changed from a scowl to surprise. She smiled and thanked me for coming back.

Scripture tells us of Jesus' love for all people. I had just mistreated someone, and the Holy Spirit showed me immediately that what I had done was wrong. Some act of repentance was necessary. On the way home I praised God for loving me enough to correct me when I stray. Viewing this person as one of God's people helped me see how wrong I was to show disrespect. I want always to show grace in the way I speak to others.

Prayer: *Dear God, help us each day to affirm the worth and dignity of those around us by our words and by our actions. Amen*

Thought for the day: Honour the presence of God in each person you meet.

Gale A. Richards (Iowa, US)

So Little?

Read Luke 9:10–17

A poor widow came and put in two very small copper coins, worth only a fraction of a penny.
Mark 12:42 (NIV)

A cell. An atom. An idea. A word. A small donation. One talent. Five loaves and two fish. Dorcas' needle. David's five stones. A quick touch of the hem of Jesus' garment. A smile. A kind word.

God has the power to take something that you and I would call little and turn it into something that becomes so much more. He has a way of multiplying our small gift, our small talent, and our small efforts and turning them into things that accomplish a great deal.

Remember the story of the boy in a large crowd with a small lunch that fed thousands? (Luke 9:10–17). The boy offered what he could; Jesus prayed over it and then used it to feed a multitude. This boy's simple lunch is something we're still talking about today.

What if we offered to God our small gifts, talents and work, if we prayed about them and asked God to use them? If we truly believe God's power is at work in us and through us, our little could do much. In fact, if we just step back and look, we may see that God has already been doing so. Looking at what God has done in our past can strengthen our resolve to make ourselves available in our future.

Prayer: *Dear God of miracles, help us always to realise that little is much when you are involved. Amen*

Thought for the day: God can do more with our little than we could do with everything.

Andy Baker (Tennessee, US)

PRAYER FOCUS: THOSE WHO FEEL THEY HAVE NOTHING TO GIVE

Faith

Read Romans 14:7–8
Those of steadfast mind you keep in peace—in peace because they trust in you.
Isaiah 26:3 (NRSV)

My mother finds out today if she has cancer. I have trouble not letting fear dominate my feelings as we wait for news that could alter our lives. I am thankful for the experiences God has brought me through thus far, chances to build my faith and to understand more fully that he is at work in all things.

Before I came to faith in Christ, my life was sometimes ruled by paralysing fear and anxiety. Panic is a familiar place, and I go there instinctively. With faith, I know that regardless of the outcome, my mother is in God's hands.

Real faith sticks it out and trusts God when life is uncertain. I pray for my mother's good health. I make sure to lift her spirit in all the ways I can, I pray for comfort in her fear, courage for my father, skill for the doctors. Most of all, I pray that my mother will feel God's love no matter what we face.

When our heart is full of anguish, we can cry out to God. We pray and then we remain still and listen. And God meets us.

Prayer: *Dear Lord, thank you for meeting us where we are. Grow our trust in you, teaching us to find comfort in your promises. When we do, provide us with opportunities to comfort others. Amen*

Thought for the day: In fearsome times, focusing on God's love can move us from panic to peace.

Christa Sterken (Indiana, US)

PRAYER FOCUS: THOSE AWAITING A MEDICAL DIAGNOSIS

The Meaning of Success

Read Matthew 6:18–21 and 2 Corinthians 5:1–10

Whether we are at home or away, we make it our aim to please [the Lord].
2 Corinthians 5:9 (NRSV)

What is success? Success to many people means having a good career, a flourishing business, a high-ranking position or great material wealth. However, these measure success from an earthly perspective. Success from the spiritual perspective is not about what people possess. All worldly 'success' will end, but our spiritual success will last for ever, into eternity.

Recently, when my uncle died, I was reminded that we are only dust. When we die, we take nothing with us from this earth. Whatever material wealth we have amassed in this life will be meaningless. Lasting accomplishment is a life characterised by deeds of love. When we live out God's will in this way, we succeed.

The day will come when each of us will be accountable before Christ for what we do in this world. I want to live in ways that please God in whatever I do. That's true success.

Prayer: *Dear God, our Father, help us to please you in whatever we do, so that you may find us faithful. Amen*

Thought for the day: A life centred on Christ is a successful life.

Marcelina Dewi Kumalasari (Jakarta, Indonesia)

Having a Good Day

Read Genesis 2:4–9

This is the day that the Lord has made; let us rejoice and be glad in it.
Psalm 118:24 (NRSV)

In the United States we usually greet each other by saying, 'Hello' or 'Hi.' Sometimes we ask, 'How are you?' though we normally don't expect an answer beyond, 'I'm fine. How are you?'

For several years now, when greeted with 'How are you?' I have often responded with 'Great! I woke up breathing this morning!' Similarly, when someone bids me, 'Have a good day', I have often responded with, 'I'm already having one! I woke up breathing this morning!' This usually brings a surprised look to the inquirer's face, followed by a smile and often a comment such as, 'Hey! That's a good way to start any day, isn't it?'

I think that my unusual response to these usual greetings causes people to reflect on the fact that any day we wake up breathing is, as Psalm 118:24 puts it, 'a day that the Lord has made', a day in which to 'rejoice and be glad'.

The creation story in Genesis says that God breathed into us the breath of life. Any day we wake up with that breath still in us is a good day, a day in which to heed the words of Psalm 150:6 which says, 'Let everything that has breath praise the Lord' (NIV).

Prayer: *Dear God, whatever we face as we wake up each morning, help us to remember that the day before us is one more day of life that you have given us. Amen*

Thought for the day: The presence of God's breath within us is cause for joy and praise.

Gus Browning (Texas, US)

New Habits

Read 2 Peter 1:3–11

As shoes for your feet put on whatever will make you ready to proclaim the gospel of peace.
Ephesians 6:15 (NRSV)

I purchased new shoes recently. From experience, I know that wearing new shoes the first few times can be painful. They may be tight or pinch a little, giving me sore toes or even a blister. But this time, as usual, I endured the pain because my old shoes were worn out and unusable. I expected that eventually the new shoes would become as comfortable as the old ones had been.

This experience reminds me of how I feel in following Christ. My attitudes or behaviour sometimes need to change. But like what happens when I lay aside old shoes for new ones, the process of changing to reflect Christ's attitudes and behaviour is not always easy—or comfortable. Yet I choose to press on until the new habits God desires to instil in me are a comfortable and ongoing part of my life.

Prayer: *Dear God, help us to be open to change as you create new life in us. We pray as Jesus taught us, saying, 'Our Father which art in heaven, Hallowed be thy name. Thy kingdom come. Thy will be done, as in heaven, so in earth. Give us day by day our daily bread. And forgive us our sins; for we also forgive every one that is indebted to us. And lead us not into temptation; but deliver us from evil.' * Amen*

Thought for the day: As I walk with Christ every day, my new life will fit better and better.

Julie White (Oregon, US)

PRAYER FOCUS: THOSE WITHOUT SHOES
* Luke 11:2–4 (KJV)

God's Teachings

Read Isaiah 2:2–4

The Lord God says, 'They will not hurt or destroy on all my holy mountain; for the earth will be full of the knowledge of the Lord as the waters cover the sea.'

Isaiah 11:9 (NRSV)

I was a teenager during the horrors of World War II. One day I said to my minister: 'I don't understand. If God is a loving God, then why are there wars, poverty, misery and other injustices?'

He answered, 'Jorge, when a person is ill and goes to the doctor, the doctor prescribes a treatment plan. How should the patient respond? First, the patient has to have confidence in the physician and then follow a treatment plan. If he does not trust the physician or follow the prescribed treatment, do you think he will be well?'

'I don't think so,' I said.

'The same happens to us. God gives us teachings to follow so there will be peace not war, and abundance not poverty, and so we can enjoy life and all God's creation. But what happens? We do not put our trust in God. We doubt his word and do not follow his teachings.'

I will never forget my pastor's words. He made it clear to me how tragic it is for us to live without God. But if instead we live the way God teaches, we can help rid the world of injustice, war and poverty.

Prayer: *Thank you, Lord, for your mercy on us sinners and for sending your Son to save us. Amen*

Thought for the day: God's word offers us wisdom to heal our countries and our world.

Jorge Roberto Rodigou (Cordoba, Argentina)

PRAYER FOCUS: COUNTRIES TORN BY WAR

Cooking for God

Read 1 Corinthians 12:4–11

There are different kinds of gifts, but the same Spirit.
1 Corinthians 12:4 (NIV)

I met two men who left jobs with regular hours and regular pay so they could open a restaurant. They wanted to put their cooking talents to work for God, using part of their income to sponsor mission trips. After the first year, the men were able to help fund such a trip. The next year, they were able to fund an entire mission trip on their own. Their restaurant is now well known for its barbecued meats and its charitable projects.

The Bible teaches that we all have talents and gifts. These men share their gifts and their profits to spread God's love. Our gifts can range from barbecuing to babysitting, from singing to smiling. Being able to share another person's heavy load is a gift.

We can use our talents wherever we are—with people, or at home praying for them. Whether we use our gifts privately or publicly, in giving of ourselves, we are enriched. In loving, we become more aware of God's great love for us and for all humankind.

Prayer: *Dear God, show us our talents that can help to spread your word and love today, and give us courage to use them often and well. Amen*

Thought for the day: Which of my talents can I use more fully for God's purposes?

Link2Life: *Show special appreciation to those who serve you when you dine out.*

Judy B. Bander (Virginia, US)

My Purpose

Read Deuteronomy 4:39–40

When you are in distress and all these things have happened to you, then in later days you will return to the Lord your God and obey him.
Deuteronomy 4:30 (NIV)

After journeying for 40 years, the Israelites reached the land God had promised them. During their years of desert wandering, they learned to trust God. He met all their needs, and they learned that obeying his commands was vital. When they rebelled, God left them to their own resources; when they realised how difficult life was without him, they returned to him, and found him waiting.

At one time I wandered around as if in a desert, as if my life had no purpose. But God never left me and was constantly drawing me into relationship. I found God most powerfully in scripture. Through reading his word daily, I found hope. I found my purpose.

That purpose is to acknowledge and obey God every day. I don't have to do something spectacular or extraordinary; I just have to walk with God in my ordinary, often unexciting life. Spending time with God every day by reading the Bible and in prayer helps me to find joy in every circumstance.

Prayer: *Dear Lord, thank you for giving us purpose and for revealing yourself to us through your word. We praise you for your mercy and steadfast love that endure for ever. Amen*

Thought for the day: When we turn to God, we have no need to wander.

Donna Miller (Colorado, US)

God is Here

Read John 16:4–7

Jesus said to the disciples, 'And remember, I am with you always, to the end of the age.'
Matthew 28:20 (NRSV)

It was my son's first day at nursery school. Before this his dad and mum had always been near, but now he was suddenly left in a noisy room with people he did not know at all. Children were crying and shouting. The teachers were trying to shout louder than all the little ones. After leaving him there, I immediately wanted to run back and stay with him. He was frightened and lonely, and he needed comfort.

At that moment, I thought that our heavenly Father longs to be with us in a fearsome world even more than I wanted to be with my son. The most joyful news is that God is with us through the Holy Spirit, our Comforter. We are not left alone in this dangerous world. Every second, with each of God's children on earth, the Spirit is present.

Having calmed down myself, I prayed that my son might also be comforted in knowing that God was beside him, even if his father and mother could not be.

Prayer: *Dear Holy Spirit, our Comforter, bring us words of love, hope, encouragement and comfort, especially when we feel alone and powerless. Amen*

Thought for the day: Stop. Turn around. God is close.

Pavel Serdukov (Moscow, Russia)

Unearthing Gold

Read Jeremiah 29:11–14

Jesus said, 'If you remain in me and my words remain in you, ask whatever you wish, and it will be given you.'
John 15:7 (NIV)

Twenty-five years ago, I asked God for the strength and willpower to overcome my addiction to cigarettes. For five years, I bounced back and forth like a pinball out of control: stopping, starting, cutting back, only to weaken later. Each time, I ended up back where I started, still smoking. Eventually, I realised that I was praying only to ask God to do something for me rather than praying to deepen my friendship with him.

To establish a relationship with God, we must get to know him personally. I began reading my Bible every morning, unearthing bits of gold about the character of God. As I grew to know God better, my objective shifted from what I wanted to what he wanted for me. First and foremost, God wants a relationship with us. As we allow his words to abide in us, we find that we are abiding in him. After that, the wonders begin.

Although it's been 20 years since I smoked my last cigarette, my journey has not been without trials. Still, I know that when we join forces with the Lord, we will find the strength we need.

Prayer: *Dear God, thank you for loving us as we are. Help us to abide in your word always. Amen*

Thought for the day: What am I doing to deepen my friendship with God?

Trudy K. Snyder (Pennsylvania, US)

Seeing Clearly

Read Mark 8:22–25

Now we see in a mirror, dimly, but then we will see face to face. Now I know only in part; then I will know fully, even as I have been fully known. And now faith, hope and love abide, these three; and the greatest of these is love.

1 Corinthians 13:12–13 (NRSV)

I have always had good vision. Some years ago, however, I realised that I was having difficulty reading. I had not read a whole book in some time. Often I would get sleepy when I would read, or my eyes would start to water from strain. One day in a department store, I saw a display of reading glasses. I tried a pair and was amazed when I could read the fine print on labels. I tried on several other pairs to find what magnification I needed to see clearly. Since then I have rediscovered the joys of reading.

Just as I needed lenses to correct my physical eyesight, I also need a lens to correct my spiritual eyesight. The Bible, the inspired word of God, is the lens we need to get a better picture of Christ. Our focus on him will correct our spiritual cloudiness and confusion. Trusting steadily in Christ and loving others extravagantly will help us see more clearly to get us through the world.

Prayer: *Dear Lord Jesus, help us to trust in you, to read your word and love others as you love us. Amen*

Thought for the day: Reading the Bible gives us a clearer picture of Christ.

Perry Louden (Tennessee, US)

Talking to God

Read Psalm 25:1–5

Jesus said, 'My sheep listen to my voice; I know them, and they follow me.'

John 10:27 (GNB)

I recently conversed with a friend who described her experiences in talking to God. I was powerfully moved when I heard about how she spent hours pouring out her deepest feelings to her Creator. I wanted to know more about her experiences and to find out what I was missing.

After several days dwelling on the matter, I took a long drive by myself. Eventually I turned off the radio and CD player and started to unload feelings that I had bottled up for a long time. I lost track of time, but I must have spent at least an hour talking to God.

Although I didn't hear God answer straight away, within in a few days I found myself trying to connect to him and listen for his voice as I prayed. I do hear God's voice inwardly now, a still small voice like that Elijah heard on Mount Horeb (see 1 Kings 19:12). At 64 years old, I ask myself, how could I have missed this all my life? I will be eternally grateful to my friend for talking to me about how she prayed. Following her example opened the door to a deeper relationship with God.

Prayer: *Dear God of the still, small voice, hear us when we pour out our hearts to you. We long to hear you speaking to us, giving your guidance for our lives. Amen*

Thought for the day: God is always ready to speak to us.

Tom Grgurich (Florida, US)

Living Alone

Read Romans 5:1–8

Praise be to… the God of all comfort, who comforts us in all our troubles, so that we can comfort those in any trouble with the comfort we ourselves have received from God.
2 Corinthians 1:4 (NIV)

When my husband died, I went to live with my son and his family for a time. Later, however, they moved to another country because of my son's business. I was left alone. Over time I grew discouraged, and self-pity was slowly taking control of me. As I prayed about my situation, I began to sense that Christ had some purpose for me.

While I was praying and waiting for guidance, I discovered a group of women who were interested in studying God's word. We began to meet, and I led them in studying the Bible. Soon I could see how obeying God's word was changing their lives. Some of them needed encouragement and counselling, and I could see the Great Counsellor and Encourager working in them.

When I read the passage from Romans 5, I better understand how God can turn our difficulties into joys if we persevere. A good way to help overcome loneliness is to make ourselves available to God—to allow him to use our hands, feet and voice to help and encourage those around us.

Prayer: *Dear Lord Jesus, when we struggle with loneliness, help us turn to you and strengthen us to reach out to others. Help us find joy and peace in you. In Jesus' name we pray. Amen*

Thought for the day: God has a purpose for each one of us.

Link2Life: *Find a way to serve someone experiencing some pain that you have faced.*

Christabel Thomas (Bangalore, India)

God's Colourful Creation

Read Genesis 1:1–31
Here there is no Greek or Jew, circumcised or uncircumcised, barbarian, Scythian, slave or free, but Christ is all, and is in all.
Colossians 3:11 (NIV)

When I was five years old, I asked my mother why people are different colours. She told me that she said a quick prayer before telling me how God wanted to create a world that was as beautiful as possible. So God filled it with rich brown soil, a brilliant yellow sun, snow-covered mountains, a velvet-black night sky and flowers more colourful than any rainbow. Then, wanting human beings to have this same colourful richness, God made some as yellow as the sun and others as black as the night sky and others as white as the snow and still others as brown as the rich earth.

I don't recall any more details of the story, but I have always remembered its essence. More than once I have thanked God that I learned at a young age that all of creation is beautiful, whether I am looking into the night sky or at my friends with their different cultural heritages.

This is one of the loveliest teachings of Christianity, that we are all God's children regardless of race or culture or any other superficial distinctions. 'Christ is all, and is in all' (Colossians 3:11). We are called to respond to each other in 'compassion, kindness, humility, gentleness and patience' (v. 12). Most of all, we are to 'put on love, which binds them all together in perfect unity' (v. 14).

Prayer: *Dear Lord, help us to recognise and cherish the beauty in your creation, especially in each person we encounter today. Amen*

Thought for the day: God must love variety, having created so much of it.

Cathemae Cecchin (California)

Navigating Life

Do you ever wish that God had built a spiritual satnav system into each of us? It would be wonderful to have audible directions and a detailed map from God for each move of every day. The satnav system I use when driving tells me exactly how far I must travel to reach my next turn, whether to bear left or right at points where I might be confused, and what time I will arrive at my destination—with continual updates as the situation changes. Having such detailed guidance is reassuring—and why I wish God had built into us a similar system spiritually. But our guidance from God is rarely direct and specific.

This is an inconvenience, to state the matter mildly. We who are serious about following Christ want to do what God wants us to do. But what does God want? To quote Hamlet (out of context), 'That is the question.' How do we discover or decide what to do in specific situations in order to be faithful?

Many would say, 'Just read the Bible.' The Bible offers us great wisdom, but it doesn't answer our specific questions about whom to marry, what profession to pursue, whether to leave a job and return to education, how to make end-of-life decisions—or many other questions. Through the centuries, however, believers have developed patterns for discerning what God wants for them—and from them—in specific situations.

One of these issues is waiting to experience either consolation or desolation in regard to a course of action. 'Consolation' is a sense of inner peace and trust as we contemplate acting; some might call it a sense of assurance. We ask God for direction, and then we prayerfully consider options one by one until one emerges as feeling 'right'. 'Desolation' is the opposite—feeling unsettled, ill-at-ease, unable to act without inner turmoil. This sense of being unsupported, inwardly perplexed, even unsafe, pulls us away from an option. As we prayerfully consider and pray about each option over time, an inward sense of unease and 'unsettledness' helps us to understand that God is pulling us away from that action.

Another way to discern guidance regarding specific decisions is what the Quakers call a 'clearness committee'. A clearness committee is a group of four or five spiritually wise, trusted people who know us well. The person seeking guidance invites individuals to be part of his or her clearness committee. The group meets for 90 minutes to a few hours. To begin the process, the person seeking guidance talks about the situation and the decision to be made, giving sufficient details to help the committee members understand the issues. Then all sit in silence. After silence, the trusted group members begin to ask questions. They do not give advice; they may only ask questions. The seeker may respond if the questions are requests for clarification, but the seeker may remain silent as well. Each question and response is followed by more silence, until all questions have been asked. The group then sits in silence until they reach consensus that all questions have surfaced. The person seeking guidance leaves the committee with a clearer sense of the important considerations, giving a basis for deciding and acting— or refraining from doing either.

A third way of discerning guidance rests with an accountability group within the faith community. An accountability group is a group of four to eight people who meet together regularly, most commonly once a week, to hold one another accountable for living their common faith and their individual calls from God. Group members covenant to pray for one another, to be honest with one another, and to support one another. Such groups may stay together for a few years or for decades. Members come to know one another deeply—their spiritual strengths and weaknesses, their continuing struggles, their closest relationships and the challenges in them, their dreams. When a group member faces a decision, others in the group talk with and pray for the person seeking guidance. Group members may ask questions, as in a clearness committee, or they may talk about times when they have faced similar dilemmas—not giving advice but providing context. They help the seeker to see the decision within the context of what they know about that person's spiritual journey and call, helping the seeker to decide for him/herself.

These methods share two characteristics: they take time, and they do not make decisions for the seeker. In the end, each of us must decide for ourselves what God is calling us to do. The support of the Christian community can help us, and we especially need their help when the decisions are important ones—but finally we must decide and act within the context of our private relationship with God. Over the last months, I have been wrestling with a difficult decision; and with the prayer support and wisdom of fellow believers, I have come to a place of consolation and clarity about my next step in life. After decades of working on *The Upper Room* magazine, I am retiring. By the time you read these words, someone new will be directing the day-to-day work of helping you listen for God's word to you through these meditations each day. I will continue to teach and to write—perhaps from time to time here in the pages of *The Upper Room*—but within a different rhythm that I look forward to with joy. I have a sense of deep consolation that I pray God will give you as you face your life decisions.

God bless each of you. You all have been an important part of my spiritual journey, and I will miss daily interaction with you. Please pray for me and for the staff of *The Upper Room* magazine as they move through this transition.

Many of the meditations in this issue address seeking and finding guidance from God. You may want to read again the meditations for September 1, 13, 16, 21, 25, 26, and 30; October 6, 13, 16, 20, 24 and 30; November 7 and 30; and December 6 as background for answering the reflection questions below.

Questions for Reflection

1. If you were convening a clearness committee to help you consider a decision, who would be on it, and why?

2. When has being part of a small group been important in your spiritual journey? What did you learn or do in the group that made it important to you?

3. What is the most momentous decision you have had to make in your life? How did you consider God's desires for you as you made it?

4. How has scripture offered you specific guidance in a time of decision? About what do you wish the Bible offered more exact guidance, and why?

5. Jesus' primary small group was the disciples. What lessons do you draw from their relationships as described in the Bible? Which of the disciples would you most like to be friends with, and why?

Mary Lou Redding

My Hero

Read Hebrews 11:1–40

As an example of patience in the face of suffering, take the prophets who spoke in the name of the Lord… You have heard of Job's perseverance and have seen what the Lord finally brought about.
James 5:10–11 (NIV)

The passages above call us to take inspiration from our fellow believers. Part of the beauty and power of growing together as the body of Christ is being in community with other people of faith. Each of us can name people who have gone before us who have challenged and encouraged us in our journey.

One of my heroes of faith grew up in a Christian home, the daughter of a minister. Her faith formed her moral and spiritual life all through high school and college and exuded from her in delightful ways. She married a deeply committed Christian man. Life was absolutely grand—until one day, while driving from her high-school teaching job, she was hit by a driver who ignored a red light. She suffered traumatic brain injury and coma. After months of therapy, she now spends life mostly in a wheelchair. Undaunted, she and her husband are rearing two children. She continues with therapy, goes on family trips and is the best friend anyone could have.

She is my daughter, Shevon, and her favourite saying is: 'Faith makes things possible, not easy.' I thank God for the blessing of Shevon and all the heroes of faith who inspire us.

Prayer: *Dear God, thank you for heroes of faith. May we strive to be one of them for others. Amen*

Thought for the day: Faith is not about having perfect life but about knowing our perfect God.

Dan Johnson (Florida, US)

Worthy

Read Romans 5:6–11

God demonstrates his own love for us in this: While we were still sinners, Christ died for us.

Romans 5:8 (NIV)

While sweeping the patio one day, I found a coin. I picked it up and noticed how grimy it was. I felt it was not worth cleaning and threw it away. Almost immediately the thought occurred to me that though the coin was thoroughly dirty, it had the same value as always.

So, too, I thought, Jesus Christ washed my sins away, and I remain a worthy child of the One who first created me. I felt sad as I thought of people whose circumstances or way of life impedes our seeing their true worth. As a result, we fail to offer them our assistance. What would have become of us if the Lord had dealt with us as I first dealt with the coin? Thanks be to God that God sees our worth and never throws anyone away.

Prayer: *Loving God, thank you for making your mercy and grace available to us. We pray as Jesus taught us, 'Our Father which art in heaven, Hallowed be thy name. Thy kingdom come. Thy will be done in earth, as it is in heaven. Give us this day our daily bread. And forgive us our debts, as we forgive our debtors. And lead us not into temptation, but deliver us from evil: For thine is the kingdom, and the power, and the glory, for ever.'* Amen*

Thought for the day: No matter how grimy we may be, we still have the same worth that God placed in us from our beginning.

Ramonita Rodríguez Sánchez (Puerto Rico)

Ready to Share

Read Acts 8:26–39

Every day in the temple and at home they did not cease to teach and proclaim Jesus as the Messiah.
Acts 5:42 (NRSV)

For many years my wife and I have made it a practice to read *The Upper Room* daily devotional guide at breakfast. Even when we are away from home we always take our copy of *The Upper Room* along with us. So when we recently went on a cruise to Mexico we continued this practice, with me reading the devotional aloud to my wife while at breakfast.

Our time of devotions attracted the attention of one of the cruise-ship's staff, who told us she had overheard the devotional for that day and that it had spoken to her. That gave us the opportunity to share our faith with her. During the course of our conversation I gave her our copy of *The Upper Room* so that she could begin her own practice of spending time with God each day. Although we were temporarily without a copy of the magazine, I knew that God would put it to good use. After that encounter we used the time we would have spent reading the devotional to pray that God's word contained in that copy of *The Upper Room* would speak in a powerful way to her.

Prayer: *Dear God, awaken us to opportunities to speak your word to those around us. Make us instruments in spreading your good news. In the name of Jesus, the source of our good news. Amen*

Thought for the day: How do I use my opportunities to spread the Good News?

Link2Life: *Introduce someone to* The Upper Room.

Mark Hrabe (Arizona, US)

In my Place

Read Romans 8:28–39
*In him we have redemption through his blood, the forgiveness of sins,
in accordance with the riches of his grace that he lavished on us with
all wisdom and understanding.*
Ephesians 1:7–8 (NIV)

The raging waters of the river were swirling under the bridge, dragging along fallen trees, boulders and mud. As he stood on the bridge, it shook under the impact of the flood. He realised that the early morning traffic crossing the bridge was in danger. In his estimation the bridge could collapse at any time.

In his uniform he stood out clearly as he placed himself on the road in the middle of the bridge. He indicated the danger and ordered the traffic to stop. Gradually the perilous situation was understood, and he was able to halt a bus and car driving onto the bridge on one side and a car and lorry approaching from the other.

The traffic waited either side of the bridge to see what would happen. What happened was disaster. Abruptly the bridge collapsed, the masonry falling into the swollen waters beneath. Into the river went his body, smashed on the rocks below. The occupants of the vehicles watched in horror. They knew that they were safe, but that he had given his life to save theirs.

Our Saviour did the same for you and me. We were headed for certain disaster and quite oblivious of the danger. Sin in our lives was leading us into destruction. He was innocent, yet he gave his life so that we could live.

Prayer: *Thank you, dear Jesus, for dying for me. Thank you for securing my eternal life. Amen*

Thought for the day: Jesus died in my place.

Carol Purves (Carlisle, England)

Slow to Speak

Read James 3:6–12

Set a guard over my mouth, O Lord; keep watch over the door of my lips.
Psalm 141:3 (NIV)

The best advice I have ever received came from my father. He told me, 'It's better to keep silent if you don't have anything kind to say,' and, 'Always use your words wisely.'

Although I watched my father live these words each day, I failed to learn from his example. Now, however, as I mature in my walk with Christ, I am finally beginning to rely on the Lord to help me, especially after my harsh words crushed a trusted friend. Once the ugly words were uttered, it was impossible to heal the wound they caused. No matter how profusely I apologised, the damage was done. Our relationship became strained and filled with tension for months. All I could do was pray, trusting God for healing and restoration. Then I waited until my friend could find it in her heart to forgive me.

I wish I had followed my father's advice and avoided this painful ordeal. Instead, I learned the hard way. Now I am more cautious and prayerful before voicing my opinions.

Prayer: *Thank you, heavenly Father, for the wisdom of our elders. Help us to learn from their example. Amen*

Thought for the day: Harsh words can wound deeply, so, be gentle when you speak.

Dorothea Love (California, US)

PRAYER FOCUS: FRIENDS WHO ARE ESTRANGED

Why do we Fear?

Read Psalm 27:1–14

[Jesus] said, 'Truly I tell you, unless you change and become like children, you will never enter the kingdom of heaven.'
Matthew 18:3 (NRSV)

When my son was four years old, I enjoyed playing a game with him. He sat on my knees, facing me. While holding him firmly by the hands, I bounced him gently. Then, without releasing his hands I stood; and still supporting him with my knees, I bent over slightly toward him, turning him upside down.

I thought he might react with apprehension; but to my surprise, he grinned. I exaggerated my movements a bit, saying, 'I think you're falling.' He continued to grin.

When I expressed my surprise at his lack of fear, he calmly responded, 'I know you won't let me fall.'

What trust! He was absolutely certain that I loved him and that I held his hands firmly. Why should he be afraid?

I never forgot his words. Jesus spoke of children for a reason. We adults fear situations that might overwhelm us. But if we hold fast to God's hand, knowing that God loves us, we have no reason to fear.

Prayer: *Loving God, we thank you for your love. Grant us the confidence that no matter what our situation is, you will not let us fall. Amen*

Thought for the day: God holds us firmly when life turns us upside down.

Elena La Puente (Buenos Aires, Argentina)

Now What?

Read Isaiah 26:1–9

Do not be conformed to this world, but be transformed by the renewing of your minds, so that you may discern what is the will of God—what is good and acceptable and perfect.
Romans 12:2 (NRSV)

The day had been much like any other until I met with my supervisor in late afternoon. The corporation where I had worked for the previous five years had decided to terminate my position. Suddenly and without notice, I was unemployed. Fear overwhelmed me; all I could think of was, 'Now what?'

Panicked and feeling betrayed, I spent the next several days focusing on my hopeless situation. Then one morning during my quiet time, two questions came to mind: What does God want me to learn from this? What new door is God about to open? Changing my thoughts of fear into anticipation put my focus back where it belonged—on God. I remembered that every overwhelming circumstance that I face in life is an invitation to become more like Christ.

Our perception of a situation can either steal or enhance the peace that God freely offers to each of us. The choice is ours: conform to the pattern of this world or allow God to renew our minds.

Prayer: *Loving Father, when life is overwhelming, you offer us peace in the middle of chaos. Help us to focus on you when we are tempted to focus on our hardships. Amen*

Thought for the day: God sometimes opens doors that we never knew existed.

Noel S. McArtor (Nevada, US)

A Different Perspective

Read Proverbs 3:1–6
Trust in the Lord with all your heart and lean not on your own understanding; in all your ways acknowledge him, and he will make your paths straight.
Proverbs 3:5–6 (NIV)

A few days ago the contents of my handbag spilled over the front seat and floor of my car. I gathered everything up and stuffed it back into my bag. Later I realised that a small plastic card I needed at work was still missing. Back in my car, I scanned the front quickly from the driver's seat and then dug through my bag again. No luck. Frustrated, I assumed I had dropped the card elsewhere and hurried off to work.

A few days later I got into my car again, but this time as a passenger. A little corner of something caught my eye, barely noticeable, peeking out of the narrow space between my seat and the centre armrest. It was the missing card! What I had needed earlier but failed to take time for was to look at my situation from a different perspective.

How often have I been guilty of the same failure to seek a different perspective in my spiritual life? By relying only on my own hasty observations, I can easily overlook what is important and right in front of me. But when I take time to slow down, read and study scripture, and open my heart to its message, God will lead me to new insights and to the answers I seek.

Prayer: *Gracious Lord, have patience and forgive us when we speed ahead, forgetting to listen to the wisdom you offer us in the Bible. Remind us to rely on the truth of your word and not simply on our own view.*

Thought for the day: The Bible offers us God's perspective on life's choices and challenges.

Elizabeth L. Easterling (Texas, US)

Fruitful

Read Matthew 9:35–38

Look around you, and see how the fields are ripe for harvesting. The reaper is already receiving wages and is gathering fruit for eternal life.
John 4:35–36 (NRSV)

Where do all these apples come from? I wondered, looking out over an orchard for the first time. Apparently, an apple contains up to ten seeds. Just imagine, if all those seeds grew into new apple trees those trees would produce apples that would produce seeds that would produce more trees and on and on. The number of trees and apples that would eventually come from one apple would be amazing.

Aren't believers supposed to be like that apple? As God renews us in the image of Christ, we are meant to bear spiritual fruit. Through the transforming power of the Holy Spirit at work in us, we can become more loving, more joyful, peaceful, patient, kind, good, faithful, gentle and self-controlled (Galatians 5:22–23). This is the fruit God wants to grow in us. And other people will see the fruit growing in us as well. Perhaps they will be attracted to Christ by the good fruit they see in us. Then the seed of our spiritual fruit can be planted and grow to produce a harvest of new believers.

Prayer: *Dear God of abundance, produce in us the fruits that you desire. Amen*

Thought for the day: God wants me to bear fruit spiritually.

Steve Wilson (Ohio, US)

The Father's Love

Read Psalm 139:1–18

[O Lord,] you know when I sit down and when I rise up; you discern my thoughts from far away. You search out my path and my lying down, and are acquainted with all my ways.
Psalm 139:2–3 (NRSV)

I hate to be apart from my daughter. Every little thing about her delights me. She is only a few days old, and her activities are limited to eating and sleeping. But still I find myself watching her endlessly. I do this because I love her immensely. I cannot get enough of looking at her.

The same kind of love is described in Psalm 139. God watches over us and knows our every move, whether we sit, stand, go out or lie down. He delights in us. He loves us and knows details about us like the number of hairs on our heads (Matthew 10:30).

But Psalm 139 is not about a God who is constantly watching us to catch us when we slip up or do something wrong. Rather, the psalm is about a loving God, who is like new parents watching their children. And it doesn't stop there, for God came to live among us, to experience life as we do and to show us the way. He wants to be intimately involved in our lives every day.

Prayer: *Loving Father, we thank you that you love us more than we can imagine and that you long to be a part of our life every day. Amen*

Thought for the day: Knowing God loves me, how will I approach this day?

Derek Sum Wei Siang (Perak, Malaysia)

Serving in Captivity

Read Daniel 1:1–7, 17–21

Paul wrote, 'I have learned to be content whatever the circumstances.'
Philippians 4:11 (NIV)

Four young men in their prime are forcibly removed from their homeland and taken to a foreign, heathen kingdom. Not only are they of noble blood; each one is gifted with intelligence and wisdom. Daniel, one of the young men, has the ability to understand dreams and visions. And it's clear from this passage that these talents are given by God.

Amazingly, the young men entered the king's service and remained there throughout Nebuchadnezzar's reign. We know from the story in the book of Daniel that these young men remained loyal in prayer and worship, serving God even while under the authority of a heathen king, even when in danger from lions or fire.

How often do we find ourselves wishing we were in a different set of circumstances? We may feel sure that we could be far more productive in a different job, a different country or a different church. Sometimes we dream of an ideal situation in which we can serve God fully. But the lesson from these young men, who could do nothing but wait on God, is to serve wherever we are, in whatever circumstances, to the best of our ability. If we are willing servants, God can use us for his divine purpose anywhere—even in captivity.

Prayer: *Dear God, help us to see beyond our circumstances to more ways we can serve you. Amen*

Thought for the day: God can use us whatever our circumstances.

Noelle Carle (Maine, US)

Tender Hearts, Gentle Words

Read Luke 10:38–42

Stand at the crossroads and look; ask for the ancient paths, ask where the good way is, and walk in it, and you will find rest for your souls.
Jeremiah 6:16 (NIV)

When I was eleven years old, I visited a school friend in his home. I knew he found arithmetic difficult, but his dad had been helping him, and he had done well in his last test. 'I baked him a chocolate cake to celebrate,' his mother told me. I was stunned. The idea of being praised for ordinary achievements was foreign to me.

My parents taught me the importance of work and of seeing each person as valuable, but some of the Christians in my church responded to emotional needs with softer hearts and gentler words than I found at home.

I also noted that in the story of Mary and Martha, Jesus praised Mary, who wasn't being productive. She needed spiritual nurture and knew that Jesus had it to give. She rebelled against custom, not working to fill the house with the smell of baking bread or to help her sister.

I've lived 70 years; and I've been like Martha at times, finding fault with people who aren't obviously productive. I also remember the sting of being criticised for reading or golfing instead of working in the garden or cleaning my room. But I pray for help to be more Christ-like in my approach to those whose values and way of living are different from mine.

Prayer: *Dear Lord, help us nurture our need to work and to find spiritual meaning, and to allow others to do the same. Amen*

Thought for the day: God loves me even when I do nothing at all.

Eugene Bales (Missouri, US)

A Greater Love

Read Lamentations 3:17–23
The steadfast love of the Lord never ceases.
Lamentations 3:22 (NRSV)

My elder son was diagnosed several years ago with schizophrenia and alcohol dependence. The complexities of his dual diagnosis include drug and alcohol abuse, homelessness, paranoia, delusional thinking and angry outbursts. We have come close to despair on many occasions. Repeatedly, we have tried to help him because we love him, but we have been forced to back away. At times I have been angry about the choices he makes that worsen his condition.

Because I'm his mother, each time I back away I feel I am a failure. I have to live with the shame and guilt that I feel because his severe mental illness is more than I can handle. My heart breaks when I think of his suffering. The sadness and sorrow of the situation at times seem too much for me to bear.

During these times, I remind myself that God is greater than my son's mental illness, my family's grief and my own helplessness and pain. I am able to get up, go to work and live with the situation for another day. I know that whatever the future holds, God's love and grace are greater than any human trial. I am able to look for today's blessings waiting for me from a God who loves my family, my son and me.

Prayer: *Loving God, bless and comfort those who struggle with mental illness. Help those who love them to cope with the trials that come with caring. Amen*

Thought for the day: God's love for us is greater than any problem we face.

Link2Life: *Offer help to someone you know who is struggling to cope.*

S. L. Ashbrooke (Virginia, US)

Exactly Where God Wants Me

Read Luke 10:25–37

Love your neighbour as yourself.

Luke 10:27 (NIV)

I find interruptions to my daily routine frustrating, especially when I'm on a tight schedule. This morning I was interrupted on several occasions. At the supermarket I encountered an assistant who was abrupt and somewhat rude. I asked him how he was, and a story of anger toward a family member came tumbling out. Later I sought out a colleague for advice. After answering my question, she tearfully told me of the recent death of her mother. At lunchtime a group of students asked if they could eat in my classroom. They had been teased, and they feared that the bullying would continue in the dining room.

But were these really interruptions? Or was I simply where God wanted me to be? Often we rush through our busy days with blinkers on, oblivious to the needs of others. Jesus commanded us to love those we meet each day. It takes little time to love our neighbour by listening, being compassionate or offering sanctuary. The supermarket assistant is my neighbour, and as I left he was smiling. My colleague is my neighbour, and she thanked me for allowing her to express her grief. My students are my neighbours, and they left their lunch break happy and more confident.

If we look at our days for opportunities to spread Christ's love to all we meet, we'll often find ourselves exactly where God intends us to be.

Prayer: *Help us, dear God, to see the interruptions of our life as opportunities to share your love. Amen*

Thought for the day: Interruptions can be opportunities to spread Christ's love.

Jill Maisch (Maryland, US)

Rejoice Always

Read Philippians 4:4–9

Paul wrote, 'Rejoice in the Lord always. I will say it again: Rejoice!'
Philippians 4:4 (NIV)

This morning I called my office to inform them that I would not be at work again today. This has happened all too frequently for more than 30 years because of chronic back pain. At times my condition fills me with anger, anxiety and hopelessness.

This morning, to take my mind off the pain, I am reading a book about homeless orphans in Kenya. They have almost no food, clothing or shelter. But their greatest pain is having no one to love them, protect them and care about them. Missionaries are able to connect with some of these young people and provide for their physical needs while they share the love of Jesus with them.

The condition of these orphans makes my physical pain seem insignificant. I have abundant shelter, food and clothing. I have the love of family and friends. Best of all, I have the privilege of knowing Christ as my Saviour. This gives me a reason to rejoice and gives me peace that passes all understanding (see Philippians 4:7). I want to help share that joy and peace with those who need it.

Prayer: *Dear Lord, when I feel overwhelmed, surround me with your presence and peace. Give me the opportunity today to share with others both materially and spiritually. Amen*

Thought for the day: We can rejoice and give thanks even during difficult times.

Link2Life: *Can you organise a collection in your church to send to needy people overseas?*

Robert M. White (Texas, US)

Cellophane Fish

Read Matthew 12:34–35

Jesus said, 'By this everyone will know that you are my disciples, if you have love for one another.'

John 13:35 (NRSV)

During the children's part of the service, the pastor placed a cellophane fish in the palm of his hand. After a few seconds he ordered the fish to jump. And it did, much to the amazement of children and adults alike. Later the pastor explained that the warmth generated by his hand caused the cellophane fish nestled within it to curve slightly, then 'jump' at the precise moment he gave the command.

Even though the pastor explained it, my four-year-old daughter commented later, 'Did you see what the pastor did? He told the little fish to jump, and the fish obeyed him!' We explained again what had happened and how. 'But the fish did obey the pastor and jump when he told it to,' she answered. Further explanation was futile. What she had witnessed spoke louder than any explanation we could offer.

We see the same dynamic as we talk about the kingdom of God and his love. No matter how eloquent our words, hearers will not be convinced when our actions speak a different message. Only when God lives in our hearts and his love is reflected in our actions will others listen to the message we proclaim.

Prayer: *Fill us with your infinite love, O God, so that your Spirit may speak and work in and through our lives. Amen*

Thought for the day: Do my actions reflect devotion to the God I profess to serve?

Graciela Kupcevich Cohen (Rio Negro, Argentina)

A Savoury Dish

Read Psalm 104:14–15, 27–30

Let us not become weary in doing good, for at the proper time we will reap a harvest if we do not give up.
Galatians 6:9 (NIV)

A few months ago, I planted a garden, eagerly anticipating the time when I would sit at the table and enjoy the taste of fresh home-grown vegetables. The hard work of preparing the soil, sowing the seeds, watering and weeding just heightened the anticipation. This reminds me of the work that God does to prepare us for harvest. He enriches the soil of our hearts by sending people into our lives to prepare the way for us to come to know Jesus Christ and commit to following him.

Of course, in my garden I might pull up a certain plant because it was not doing as well as the others. At other times I destroy some plants because I am too careless while weeding. I am so glad that the Lord is not like me! In great love, God tends our souls and gives us what we need.

Today I reaped some of the produce of my garden. Thinking of the savoury dish I will soon enjoy from my garden's produce makes me thankful I did not give up when the days were hot and the weeds seemed out of control. The work I put into my harvest makes me appreciate all that God does for us. He will never give up on tending our souls.

Prayer: *Most holy and gracious God, thank you for not giving up on us and for meeting our every need. Help us to persevere so that you will have an acceptable harvest through us. Amen*

Thought for the day: Remembering all that God does for us strengthens us to keep going.

Leon McBride (Georgia, US)

God's Ways

Read Isaiah 55:6–11

O the depth of the riches and wisdom and knowledge of God! How unsearchable are his judgments and how inscrutable his ways!
Romans 11:33 (NRSV)

Many years ago, I wrote a meditation for *The Upper Room* on the issue of conflict. Several months later, the editor emailed me. She had liked my theme but didn't think the scripture text I had selected was appropriate. She suggested I attempt a rewrite. After some thought, I selected Psalm 4:4, 'In your anger do not sin; when you are on your beds, search your hearts and be silent' (NIV).

Just hours later, someone let me down. Even as anger began to boil within me, the words I had meditated on that morning sprang to mind. I also remembered the 'Thought for the Day' I had penned: 'Before you speak, let the word speak to you.' By heeding the command and counsel of Psalm 4:4, I was able to deal with my anger without attacking the other person.

Afterwards, I praised God for bringing together that request for a rewrite and the psalmist's words from Psalm 4. Against the background of God's leading, I was able to meditate on that verse and apply its truth as I faced that day's events. Incidentally, I never saw that particular meditation in print; but the lesson God taught me that morning is etched on my heart.

Prayer: *Dear Father, thank you for the many ways you teach us. Keep us open to your truth. Amen*

Thought for the day: God speaks to us in many—sometimes mysterious—ways.

Link2Life: *Have a try at writing your own Upper Room meditation.*

Tanya Ferdinandusz (Western Province, Sri Lanka)

PRAYER FOCUS: THOSE STRUGGLING WITH A HOT TEMPER

A Lesson in Forgiveness

Read Ephesians 4:30–32

Be kind and compassionate to one another, forgiving each other, just as in Christ God forgave you.
Ephesians 4:32 (NIV)

Several months ago, I was playing a card game with my nephew. While we played the game, I remembered how he had been wrongly accused of doing something at school, and I reminded him of it. From my point of view, my nephew had a right to be angry about being treated unjustly. But he wasn't angry at all, and his forgiveness was quick. 'It's OK, they make mistakes.'

Sometimes our pain goes a lot deeper than being falsely accused, and sometimes forgiveness can feel impossible! But God never gives us a command without giving us grace and strength to obey it.

My nephew's example encourages me to be as forgiving as he is. With God's grace and strength, I can forgive others as Christ has forgiven me.

Prayer: *Dear God, when someone hurts us, help us to remember how much you have forgiven us. Take our pain and give us your grace to forgive others as you have forgiven us, as we pray, 'Father, hallowed be your name, your kingdom come. Give us each day our daily bread. Forgive us our sins, for we also forgive everyone who sins against us. And lead us not into temptation.'* Amen*

Thought for the day: Forgiveness frees both the one being forgiven and the one who forgives.

Tyler Myers (Ohio, US)

PRAYER FOCUS: PEOPLE WRONGLY ACCUSED
* Luke 11:2–4 (NIV)

God in Us

Read Genesis 1:27–31

God created humankind in his image, in the image of God he created them; male and female he created them.

Genesis 1:27 (NRSV)

I grew up without a healthy self-image. As a result, I competed in everything, trying to prove myself worthy while believing that most people had many more talents and gifts than I. When a major crisis came into my life, I didn't think I could endure those thoughts anymore. At that point, I thought of suicide. Then, through the power of the Holy Spirit, I found healing in my heart. I felt new.

After being drawn to God's holy word, the Bible, I read the above scripture many times without realising its meaning. But as I studied the verse with others and surrendered to what God wanted to me to hear, I became whole, realising that my worth comes not from what I do but from how I was created.

Nothing I can say, do or accomplish compares to knowing that I am created in God's image. Life with its ups and downs will try to strip this assurance from us. But every time we read the above verse, we can remember how valuable we are and how much God loves us.

Prayer: *Dear Creator and sustainer of all things, thank you for creating us in your likeness. Amen*

Thought for the day: Because we bear God's image… each of us has unlimited value.

Tim Wymbs (Pennsylvania, US)

The Best Words of All

Read Psalm 19:7–14

Oh, how I love your law! It is my meditation all day long.
Psalm 119:97 (NRSV)

When I was growing up, the highlight of our week was Friday when Mother bought six sweet buns from the bakery, one for each member of the family. It was the best of weekend treats! As I stepped into the shop with her, I always read the Bible quotation that was framed outside the door—Romans 5:8: 'God demonstrates his own love for us in this: While we were still sinners, Christ died for us.' Even though I was quite young, the words impressed me and I remembered them long after we moved away.

Some years later, I met a friend who was a 'memory verse' enthusiast. As I rode on the back of her motor scooter, she would call out the first half of a verse and wait for me to complete it. Now I've memorised quite a number of verses, and I like to recall them as I fall asleep or when I wake in the morning. Sometimes they come to mind when I'm waiting in a queue or enjoying a walk. They are also a great help when I need the right words to complete a letter or card. More than once I've found myself saying, 'Thank you, Lord, that I can use your words for the end of this note. They're so much better than mine!'

It's exciting to realise that there are many more verses yet to discover and memorise. I'll never come to the end of them all, nor can anyone ever take them away from me. The psalmist put it well: the words of God are 'sweeter than the purest honey' (Psalm 19:10, GNB).

Prayer: *O Lord, make us hungry every day for your word, and help us to feed on it. Amen*

Thought for the day: God's word stored in our hearts is a lasting treasure.

Elaine Brown (Perthshire, Scotland)

Before We Vanish

Read Deuteronomy 8:11–20
What is your life? For you are a mist that appears for a little while and then vanishes.
James 4:14 (NSRV)

I'll never forget my first real job—the excitement of responsibility, the energy of new colleagues, the first pay-cheque with so much promise. As long as the money kept coming in, the job felt more like play than work. I was happier than I'd been in a long time. But it wasn't long until that excitement, energy and promise gave way to the world of family, bills and those unexpected circumstances that keep us awake all night.

The moment I felt confident enough to buy something 'for me', small disasters struck—the car needed mending or the washing machine broke down. Soon I began to feel as if bad things would always happen at the exact time my money started making me comfortable and happy. It's easy to take pride in financial gain. Pride can lead to arrogance, and having money can make us feel as if we have no need for God.

Certainly we are called to give thanks for what we have, but all of it is only mist. The sobering question from James always remains: 'What is your life?' While that thought may be daunting, we are comforted with the thought that God is much greater than, and gives more comfort than, any amount of money or possessions.

Prayer: *Teach us, Father, to boast not in our wealth, but in you. Amen*

Thought for the day: What shall I do with my wealth before it—and I—vanish?

Billy Collins (Texas, US)

The Next Generation

Read Genesis 45:1–28

Then, still weeping, [Joseph] embraced each of his brothers and kissed them. After that, his brothers began to talk with him.
Genesis 45:15 (GNB)

When we answered the telephone, we were excited to hear our four-year-old grandson's voice. After telling us about nursery school, he said, 'I need to ask you a question: why didn't God help Joseph's brothers when they were hungry?' We had talked about Joseph when our grandson was at our holiday Bible club. Our grandson remembered that Joseph's brothers had taken Joseph's coat without his permission and had put him in a pit.

I said that God did help Joseph's brothers by leading them to Joseph. Since Joseph worked for the king, he was able to give them food and a place to live. Also, I told him that God helped Joseph to forgive his brothers even though they were afraid that Joseph was still angry with them.

He seemed satisfied with my answer and gave his mum the phone. She said they had discussed Joseph recently at Sunday school. Regardless of his reasons for asking, I realised again the joy of being able to follow God's word in Psalm 78:4: 'We will tell the next generation about the Lord's power and his great deeds and the wonderful things he has done.'

Prayer: *Thank you, God, for opportunities to talk about you with our children and grandchildren. Amen*

Thought for the day: All children need relationships with adults who will help them learn God's stories and his ways.

Dan W. Moore (North Carolina, US)

In Step

Read Psalm 13:1–6

I sought the Lord, and he answered me, and delivered me from all my fears.

Psalm 34:4 (NRSV)

Every morning I practise a gentle exercise routine that helps my ageing joints to keep working. I have found music to fit in with my movements, which makes the practice even more enjoyable. This morning, I realised that I was out of step with the music. For a few moments I had lost my concentration, and it had all gone wrong. I had to start again.

This reminded me of how I feel when other things go wrong and I feel out of step with what is happening. My son's cancer, my daughter's marriage break-up and my declining health have all happened quite suddenly and shaken my world. I did not always choose the best ways of coping in these situations. One way in which I responded—withdrawing from my normal activities and keeping my pain locked up inside me—did not help me regain my balance.

Thankfully, I now know that having a personal relationship with God, praying about my sorrows and pain and putting my trust in him, will carry me through the bad times. God sets me back on track. And when I keep in step with him, I can keep my balance even when events shake me.

Prayer: *Thank you, Lord, for always being with us, so that when we face difficulties we can turn to you for help. Amen*

Thought for the day: Trusting God helps us keep our balance in a chaotic world.

Shirley Smith (Hertfordshire, England)

PRAYER FOCUS: FAMILIES FACING GREAT CHANGE

Speaking Truth in Love

Read Ephesians 4:11–16

Agree with one another, live in peace; and the God of love and peace will be with you.
2 Corinthians 13:11 (NRSV)

The words quoted above follow Paul's expression of concern that in his forthcoming visit he would find the same problems he had already identified in his first letter to the church at Corinth. The Corinthian believers had allowed certain teachings to divide them, making some factions believe themselves to be more holy and worthy than others.

This reminds me of a colleague who attends a different church from mine. I like him, and we work well together. But when we talk about our beliefs, I always come away feeling that he views my faith and my church as second-rate Christianity. He always implies that the worship and spiritual practices at my church are not good enough. He ends every discussion by inviting me to his church.

Through the words of Paul the apostle, God calls me to discover how to speak truthfully to my colleague in ways he can hear, to build bridges rather than to carry resentment. This reading teaches us to live in peace with one another so the grace of Christ Jesus and the friendship of God will be with us and be seen in us.

Prayer: *Holy God, bring us the friendship with you that helps us work out the issues that separate us from one another and from you. Amen*

Thought for the day: 'Blessed are the peacemakers, for they will be called children of God' (Matthew 5:9).

David William McKay (Ontario, Canada)

An Illusion?

Read Jeremiah 31:31–34

David prayed, 'O Lord God, you are God, and your words are true.'
2 Samuel 7:28 (NRSV)

My dad has always been able to cut through trivial issues to the heart of a matter. Knowing how I love to backpack but concerned for my safety, he once asked, 'Do you think a lightweight nylon tent will protect you from wild animals?' I joked that it was rather like toddlers playing peek-a-boo, covering their eyes and declaring, 'You can't see me!' But in fact a tent doesn't offer real protection from animals, merely the illusion of safety.

Looking back, I realised that for many years I had treated the Bible in much the same way, assuming that merely having one and occasionally reading it would guarantee my spiritual well-being. However, the story of King David caused me to re-evaluate my attitude. David professed his devotion to God, but his profession was severely compromised by his affair with Bathsheba. When his sin was revealed, David realised that he had displeased God and repented (2 Samuel 11—12).

Simply carrying a Bible or saying that I love it offers only an illusion of spiritual security. Real spiritual security comes from a relationship with God, allowing the message of scripture to sink into our spirit to make us more like Christ.

Prayer: *Heavenly Father, may the sincerity of our obedience match the intensity of our professions of faith. Amen*

Thought for the day: What we believe is revealed more through behaviour than words.

Thomas Dury (Colorado, US)

More Than a Teacher

Read Philippians 3:7–11

As he went ashore, he saw a great crowd; and he had compassion for them, because they were like sheep without a shepherd; and he began to teach them many things.

Mark 6:34 (NRSV)

I am amazed at how fans sometimes go to extremes to see their favourite celebrities. When a popular celebrity stages a concert in Manila, people from the farthest provinces try diligently to get there. When my favourite Christian band came to the Philippines for the first time, I saved money for tickets, reserved seats for my best friend and myself, and got my boss's approval to leave early so I could attend the concert.

This experience reminded me of the 5,000 people who went out to see Jesus. Imagine thousands of people from different places travelling on foot to see and hear the famous teacher. The crowds who followed Jesus wanted to make sure they could see him and hear him teach personally. But unlike many celebrities today, Jesus was never pretentious. Perhaps he even looked like any common person of that period. I wonder what it was about Jesus that made multitudes of people follow him?

Jesus said, 'I am the light of the world' (John 8:12). His wisdom and compassion attracted people wherever he went. People wanted to know him more and to witness his works of mercy. May we too follow Jesus, no matter where we are. He is more than a prophet and a teacher; he is our Lord and Saviour who sacrificed himself for us.

Prayer: *O God, make us hunger to know you more. Refresh us with your love and grace that we may adore you always. Amen*

Thought for the day: Who or what do you seek most in life?

Rhema Joy Penaflor (Bulacan, Philippines)

A Simple Prayer

Read Psalm 28:6–9

The Lord says, 'You will seek me and find me when you seek me with all your heart.'
Jeremiah 29:13 (NIV)

At times I am sure of God's presence; I feel his love; I understand his will for me. But in other, desert times I feel cold and distant, far from God's light and guidance. When I pray during those times, I feel as if I am speaking to the walls.

Still, every night I pray with my 13-year-old son. My son is not so willing as he once was to pray aloud, but we give thanks for the people and events for which we are most grateful each day. It is a lovely way to close the day, welcome the night and enter into rest.

One recent night, my life seemed to be spinning out of control. I am a single parent. I was unemployed, and even losing the battle with daily household chores. All I could think to pray was, 'Help!' My son was delighted; he thought 'Help' was a wonderful prayer, simple and to the point.

So I prayed 'Help'—for my mum in her fight with acute leukae-mia, for the family of a man who had recently suffered multiple strokes overnight and then died, and for my prayer partner who was recovering from her second knee surgery. God lifted each burden from my heart as I prayed one word: Help. By the time I had finished praying, I felt reconnected to God. Like the psalmist, 'I call on the Lord in my distress, and he answers me' (Psalm 120:1).

Prayer: *Dear God, help! Amen*

Thought for the day: If we ask, God will help.

Gloria Graves Gregory (Tennessee, US)

PRAYER FOCUS: CHILDREN OF SINGLE PARENTS

Growing in Grace

Read Joshua 5:10–15

The manna ceased on the day they ate the produce of the land.
Joshua 5:12 (NRSV)

While the children of Israel wandered in the wilderness, manna fell from heaven to sustain them each day. Once they entered the promised land, the manna ceased to fall and they became responsible for producing their own food. As with the Hebrews, at times, God supplies our needs without any effort on our part. When blessings come in this way, recognising and celebrating the grace of God is easy.

However, God is still at work when we enter a different phase of life where we must participate in realising God's blessings. I've seen both types of grace in the various stages of my career. My first two jobs came to me with little effort on my part. In seeking a third position, I had several interviews and suffered multiple rejections. After starting the job, difficult circumstances made me start thinking that the job wasn't going to work out. However, these experiences built in me qualities of character, resilience and confidence for which I came to thank God. I saw his grace to me when it was easy to find work. Then, I saw his grace grow richer and fuller when the position came after initial disappointment and much effort.

As loving parents want to see their children mature and take on responsibility, so God, our loving father, wants us to grow in grace. That effort is required of us does not mean that God's love is diminished. Being faithful through our work and our struggles shows gratitude for the grace of God.

Prayer: *God of grace, help us to understand the ways you want to work with us, in us and through us. Amen*

Thought for the day: Surviving our struggles is a testimony to God's grace.

William Smith (Virginia, US)

Light Check

Read Matthew 5:13–16

Jesus said, 'Let your light shine before others, so that they may see your good works and give glory to your Father in heaven.'
Matthew 5:16 (NRSV)

For more than five years I have used a lift that has a burned-out light in the panel indicating floor numbers. Each time I enter the lift I press the third-floor button, expecting it to illuminate. Instead, it is dim. So I press the button again, thinking perhaps I didn't press hard enough. Still it remains dark. Glancing at the panel on the other side of the lift, I see that the third-floor button is lit, confirming that the elevator will stop on the floor I want it to even though the button I pressed is dark. I relax, confident that I am headed where I want to go because the light tells me so.

The working and non-working lights remind me of two important aspects of my faith journey. First, if I am to go forward with confidence to my desired destination, my path must be illumined with the Lord's light to guide me in all situations. When I stray from the light, I falter and my path is difficult to follow. Second, I must take care that my light is shining every day. If I profess to be a Christian but the light of Christ does not shine from me, how can others be drawn to Christ?

The lights in the lift remind me to complete a personal 'light check'. Am I walking in the Lord's light, and am I projecting that light into the world?

Prayer: *Dear Lord, especially as we approach the season of Advent, help us to reflect your light into the world, offering hope to those who are hurting and in need. Amen*

Thought for the day: How am I bringing God's light to the world?

Jacquelynn Leggett (Virginia, US)

Abba, Daddy

Read Mark 14:32–42

You did not receive a spirit of slavery to fall back into fear, but you have received a spirit of adoption. When we cry, 'Abba, Father!' it is that very Spirit bearing witness with our spirit that we are children of God.
Romans 8:15-16 (NRSV)

'Daddy, I need you' woke me from a deep sleep. I went to see what my daughter wanted. A drink of water and some reassuring words allayed her fears, and she fell back to sleep. I remained awake, struck by the simple word 'daddy'. Daddy is a name that is earned; it comes from a relationship and is not just a matter of information. Anyone can be a father, but to be called 'Daddy' requires an investment of time and a true bond. A child who calls for her daddy knows that someone she can trust, someone who loves her, will respond.

When Jesus was facing crucifixion, he cried out to his daddy. *Abba* is Aramaic for 'daddy'. When Jesus was in the garden, praying to his Father, he cried out, '*Abba*, Father'. He asked that the cup of death be taken from him, but continued, saying, 'Yet not what I will, but what you will' (Mark 14:36, NIV).

When we commit to Christ, we become children of God. As we invest time in our relationship with God, we come to call out, '*Abba*, Daddy,' asking for help and knowing that God will respond with love.

Prayer: *Dear God, thank you for being our daddy, whom we can trust to respond in love. Amen*

Thought for the day: What name for God holds special meaning for you, and why?

Matthew Reger (Ohio, US)

Never Alone

Read Luke 1:46–55

The virgin will be with child and will give birth to a son, and they will call him 'Immanuel'—which means 'God with us.'
Matthew 1:23 (NIV)

The Christmas season is a time of conflicting emotions for me. My husband died just two days after Christmas, and, even after all these years, I clearly remember how I felt coming home from the hospital—seeing the holly wreath brightening our door and the Christmas tree sparkling in our living room. I remember thinking that all that colour and festivity seemed almost obscene on this, the worst day of my life. That afternoon I took everything down and packed it away. I have never regained any interest in decorating for Christmas.

On the other hand, the true meaning of Christmas has become very precious to me. It's the day we celebrate the birth of Jesus, our Lord and Saviour. My relationship with Christ has become closer and more comforting as time has passed, and I have come to trust and cling to his promises: 'Come to me, all you that are weary and are carrying heavy burdens, and I will give you rest' (Matthew 11:28, NRSV). 'I will not leave you comfortless: I will come to you' (John 14:18, KJV).

I don't decorate my home with lights and garlands or decorate a Christmas tree. People who don't know me may think I don't celebrate Christmas; but I do. Instead of gifts and feasting, I set aside that day to reflect on all that the birth of Jesus means to me. I am not alone. I will never be alone. That is the precious gift of Christmas.

Prayer: *Heavenly Father, thank you for your assurance that in our loneliness and sorrow, you are always here to comfort us. Amen*

Thought for the day: Christmas means we are never alone.

Ruby Truax (Ontario, Canada)

PRAYER FOCUS: THOSE MOURNING THIS CHRISTMAS

Hiking in the Dark

Read Psalm 119:105–112

Your word is a lamp to my feet and a light for my path.
Psalm 119:105 (NIV)

For many years I was a Boy Scout leader. I enjoyed teaching young boys about the outdoors. There is much to learn about living in and moving through forests and woodlands. Having the right equipment and knowing how to use it can mean the difference between sleeping in a warm tent, and shivering all night in cold, wet bedding. I've done both, and believe me, it is much nicer to be warm and dry.

Sometimes the boys and I would drive to one area to camp and then hike to our final campsite. Invariably, someone would leave something important back in the cars. And almost always it wasn't until dark that the forgotten article was missed or needed.

Recovering the needed article always involved a trip back to the car park… in the dark. So out came the torch. After a number of those treks in the dark, I realised that God's word is something like that torch of mine. God promised a light for my path—just enough light to help me take the next few steps to where I am going. I need to know that God leads me. I need to trust him. I need to remember that his grace is sufficient for all my days.

Today and every day in the words of scripture God gives 'a lamp to my feet and a light for my path'.

Prayer: *Thank you, O Lord, for giving us what we need today. Thank you for your light that shines on us no matter how dark our path may become. Amen*

Thought for the day: God gives us light for a few steps at a time.

Michael Morelan (Alabama, US)

PRAYER FOCUS: SOMEONE ON ONE OF LIFE'S DARK PATHS

A Gift of Warmth

Read Luke 12:22–31

[Jesus] said to his disciples, '… do not worry about your life, what you will eat, or about your body, what you will wear. For life is more than food, and the body more than clothing.'
Luke 12:22–23 (NRSV)

One Christmas when my children were young and I was a single parent attending college, an anonymous donor or donors provided Christmas gifts for my family. Among the gifts was a snowsuit for my three-year-old son, who loved to play in the snow. I remember the first time he came inside after playing in his new snowsuit. As I took off the coat, I could feel the warmth of his body still in the fibres of the coat. I realised that I had never before felt his warmth so strongly. Tears came to my eyes as I realised that he had finally been warm enough when playing in the snow. I gave thanks to God for the generosity of those strangers who provided for my little boy.

Now I am in a position to help others who may be struggling to be warm or to eat or to go to college. While Jesus told us not to worry about what we will eat or what we will wear, I know from personal experience that it is easier not to worry when someone comes along to help us in our struggles. By God's guidance and with God's help, we can help others to live with fewer worries. We can show them by our acts of love and care that God's love is the answer to any worry and fear.

Prayer: *Dear Father, help us to comfort others in their worries as you comfort us. Amen*

Thought for the day: God's love is made visible in our acts of generosity.

Link2Life: *Is there a family you can help this Christmas?*
Susan I. Shelso (Minnesota, US)

Turning toward Forgiveness

Read Matthew 18:15–20

If you forgive others their trespasses, your heavenly Father will also forgive you.

Matthew 6:14 (NRSV)

Forgiving is hard. In the past when I read Matthew 18:15–20, I would identify immediately with those who had been wronged. I thought Jesus had validated my feelings of being wronged and given me a model that would allow me to extract the confession and apology I deserved.

However, with time, experience, Bible study, support from Christian friends and the help of the Holy Spirit I have gained a new perspective. The reading above from Matthew 18 isn't about my wrongs being validated or my hurts being righted. It is a model for moving beyond ourselves and extending Christian love to those who may have lost their way.

But even with this new perspective, I still struggle with forgiveness and the responsibility I have as a Christian: forgive another or confess my own failures, be accountable or hold accountable. As time passes, I'm getting better at recognising which I need to do. When we focus on God and not solely on our feelings, we can respond to others with Christian love. When we look to the Holy Spirit for guidance and direction, we can reflect the example of Christ to others.

Prayer: *Forgiving God, help us to love and forgive readily, as we pray, 'Our Father in heaven, hallowed be your name, your kingdom come, your will be done on earth as it is in heaven. Give us today our daily bread. Forgive us our debts, as we also have forgiven our debtors. And lead us not into temptation, but deliver us from the evil one.'* Amen*

Thought for the day: As we forgive, God forgives us.

Rick Beck (Kentucky, US)

* Matthew 6:9–13 (NIV)

A New Beginning

Read Romans 8:5–14

All who are led by the Spirit of God are children of God.
Romans 8:14 (NRSV)

Every morning on my way to work I drive past a corner shop situated above the busiest section of the city. Usually before 8:00 am, the owner of the business stands outside on the pavement, exchanging cheerful greetings with passersby. Many of these are pupils on their way up to a primary school located on the slopes of the mountain just above the centre of the city of Cape Town, South Africa.

On one particular morning I witnessed the shop owner helping two young ones cross the street. The children laughed as he playfully pretended to give them a gentle push to help them on their way. This act of kindness and care reminded me of a shepherd keeping a watchful eye on his sheep.

In this season of Advent, we remember that God is always with us—watching over us, guiding us and giving us a sense of security, just as the shop owner on the corner brings a sense of assurance to those school children each day. Especially at this time of year, we yearn for God's guiding Spirit to give us open hearts and minds to change whatever in our lives needs changing. Advent reminds us that God is always with us, helping us to become more like Christ.

Prayer: *Dear God, in preparation for the birth of Jesus in our hearts, we pray for the gift of a new beginning where we need it most. Amen*

Thought for the day: Where do I sense God's guiding Spirit today?

Link2Life: *Get to know your local shopkeepers.*

Beatrice Smith (Western Cape, South Africa)

PRAYER FOCUS: NEIGHBOURHOOD BUSINESS OWNERS

The Power of God

Read Matthew 2:1–15

[The Lord] said to me, 'My grace is sufficient for you, for power is made perfect in weakness.' So, I will boast all the more gladly of my weaknesses, so that the power of Christ may dwell in me.

2 Corinthians 12:9 (NRSV)

The Advent season presents a stark contrast between the lust for power and greed and the call to faith. I feel we are bombarded with accounts of a seemingly never-ending stream of corruption and lies. I wonder if any integrity or anyone I can trust is left in the world. The message of Advent seems like a straw in the wind.

But the stories of Jesus' birth remind me that the days of Herod were no different from today. What chance did Joseph and Mary have against the cruelty of Herod, the powerful ruler appointed by the Roman Empire? The odds were stacked against two ordinary people with no connections, from a nowhere town. To make matters worse, the magi tipped off Herod, telling him about the coming of a king. But still God's will was accomplished.

God chooses weakness to demonstrate divine power. The Lord spoke to Paul, saying, 'My grace is sufficient for you, for my power is made perfect in weakness.' The eternal symbol of this principle is the Christ Child born into a dangerous and threatening world. Jesus showed us that what looks like weakness can be used by God.

Prayer: *Dear God, strengthen our faith daily by the knowledge that in our weakness your power is perfected. Amen*

Thought for the day: God uses our weakness to bring truth to life and bring life to truth.

Bud Lawing (North Carolina, US)

No Comparison

Read Romans 12:4–13

Paul said, 'I can do everything through [Christ] who gives me strength.'
Philippians 4:13 (NIV)

As a teacher, I have observed that not all students are good academically. Instead, they may be good at sport, art, cooking or repairing things. God has given each of us at least one talent. Therefore, we don't have to be discouraged. By focusing on what we can do, we can 'serve God' in at least one area and enjoy it.

Reflecting on this, I thought of the peacock. It has a squawky voice, but it also has a colourful tail to display. On the other hand, the nightingale has dull and unattractive feathers but can sing beautifully. Similarly, we are a mixture of traits. We can focus on what we can do instead of comparing our weakness with someone else's strength. If we lack confidence, we can always remind ourselves of the affirmation in Philippians 4:13: 'I can do everything through [Christ] who gives me the strength.'

Each of us can use our talent to glorify God.

Prayer: *Father God, thank you for blessing each of us with ability that we can use for your glory, as we pray. 'Our Father which art in heaven, Hallowed be thy name. Thy kingdom come. Thy will be done, as in heaven, so in earth. Give us day by day our daily bread. And forgive us our sins; for we also forgive every one that is indebted to us. And lead us not into temptation; but deliver us from evil.'* Amen*

Thought for the day: In what way do I most enjoy serving God?

Mary Ng Shwu Ling (Singapore)

PRAYER FOCUS: THOSE WHO FEEL THEY HAVE NO TALENTS

* Luke 11:2–4 (KJV)

The Dawn from on High

Read Luke 1:5–24, 57–80

Zechariah prayed, 'By the tender mercy of our God, the dawn from on high will break upon us, to give light to those who sit in darkness and in the shadow of death, to guide our feet into the way of peace.'
Luke 1:78–79 (NSRV)

We spent our Christmas holiday with our family. Other than playing with the grandchildren, there's nothing better than watching the sun rise over the lake—it's absolutely spectacular. But I can easily miss it by being busy reading or simply sleeping in. The sun will rise; I cannot cause it or control it. But I choose whether I will be awake to experience it. The Christmas story is as simple, and as difficult, as that.

The Christmas gospel is the shocking, unbelievable, radically reorienting story of the way God comes to be with us in Jesus Christ. Humans didn't think this up. We would never have gone searching for a God who would do something like this. We can no more 'find God' than we can cause the sun to rise. God comes to find us. The incarnation is the intrusive story of the God who comes to us like dawn breaking into the darkness of our world, in order to lead our feet into the ways of peace. We can, however, miss the dawn if we aren't awake to see it.

In Christ, God comes to be with us. We can't cause or control it. But we can miss the whole thing unless we practise the spiritual disciplines—such as prayer, Bible study and worship—that enable us to be awake to experience it. The purpose of Advent is to prepare us to be awake when the dawn comes.

Prayer: *Holy God, we wait in great expectation to experience all you offer us through your Son, Christ Jesus. Amen*

Thought for the day: Christmas is coming. Are you awake?

Jim Harnish (Florida, US)

Sowing in Sorrow

Read Psalm 126:1–6

Those who go out weeping, bearing the seed for sowing, shall come home with shouts of joy.
Psalm 126:6 (NRSV)

Clearing out my father's house after his death was a daunting and depressing task. Packing up my father's personal possessions felt like removing tangible evidence of his existence. I hugged his clothes and caressed his books before donating them to charity.

Then I opened the bathroom cabinet and stared at unopened boxes of soap, bottles of shampoo, conditioner, mouthwash, packs of razors and tubes of toothpaste, wondering what to do with them. Then I recalled reading an article in the newspaper about a homeless shelter with an ongoing need for these items, so I contacted the shelter.

That phone call inspired a ministry. I enlisted people in my church to help supply these items. On what would have been my father's 78th birthday, we made the first delivery. The generosity of our church members overwhelmed me as boxes of items were carried into the shelter. God used my grief to spur ministry to those in need; he used my pain to propel me toward a purpose I never would have imagined.

Helping those with needs far greater than my own brought me comfort and healing. I smiled, feeling my sorrow subside when homeless men thanked me for the gifts. God taught me that sowing in tears can bring a harvest of joy.

Prayer: *O Lord, help us use our sorrows to sow seeds of faith and hope to those in need. Amen*

Thought for the day: God can use even death to bring life and purpose.

Debra Pierce (Massachusetts, US)

PRAYER FOCUS: THOSE WORKING WITH HOMELESS PEOPLE

As Little Children

Read Mark 10:13–16
The kingdom of God belongs to such as these.
Mark 10:14 (NIV)

I have often wondered why we love Christmas so much. Is it because as Christians we like to celebrate the hope which Jesus' birth offers us? Is it the giving and receiving of gifts which demonstrates our love for each other? Is it that we relish the spirit of the season?

Perhaps it is a combination of all these elements. However, underlying them is the fact that at Christmastime we all get to feel like little children again. We become excited at the prospect of sharing time with our families and friends. Despite advancing age adults can still enjoy the anticipation of seeing the joy on another's face when they see the gift we selected especially for them. If it is a white Christmas, we thrill at the sight of the first snowflakes as they fall, recalling the time when we built snowmen and had snowball fights when we were young.

Let us resolve that, after all the baubles have been stored away until next Christmas, we remember we all are God's children, that we will accept all he wants to give us with gracious thanks, and in return we will show our love for him and for all people—all year round.

Prayer: *Heavenly Father, may your Spirit help us to be childlike, and may we accept your love for us at Christmas and always. Amen*

Thought for the day: How can I keep the spirit of Christmas alive all year round?

Betty Madill (Aberdeenshire, Scotland)

Something to Pray For

Read 1 Thessalonians 5:14–18
The prayer of a good person has a powerful effect.
James 5:16 (GNB)

Some days I wake up praying and go to sleep praying. Other days I think, I don't really have anything to pray about today. Then all it takes is a few moments of reflection for me to realise that whether everything is moving along smoothly or falling apart in my grasp, there is always something to pray about.

Days that flow smoothly are a great time to be thankful and to pray for others who are suffering. I can ask God what I can do this day to help a friend or neighbour. Maybe it is my turn to be the answer to someone else's prayer. We pray readily when life seems to be falling apart and we feel unable to change our situation. But our prayers can change our circumstances. God still answers prayers, every day.

Whether I need an answer to my prayers or I can be the answer to someone else's prayers, I need to pray. Prayer changes everything!

Prayer: *Dear Lord, in good times and in bad, we praise you for all that you are doing in our lives. Help us to reach out to those for whom we pray. Amen*

Thought for the day: Today I can be the answer to someone's prayer.

Link2Life: *Pray for each person you meet today.*

Susan Scott (Texas, US)

The Christmas Coat

Read Ephesians 2:4–10

You have stripped off the old self with its practices and have clothed yourselves with the new self, which is being renewed in knowledge according to the image of its creator.

Colossians 3:9–10 (NRSV)

In mid-December, a couple came into the gift shop where I work. As I helped them, I also commented on the woman's beautiful coat. After chatting for a few moments, the couple continued to browse. Soon the gentleman approached me with the coat and asked me to try it on. When I told him I couldn't do that, he announced, 'This is for you! Merry Christmas!' He thrust it at me; and the couple made a quick getaway, before I could find out their names or even thank them.

This experience of extravagant generosity caused me to reflect on God's gift of salvation. The coat was a gift. I had done nothing to deserve it. God gives us the greatest gift, salvation through Jesus Christ, which cannot be earned. Also, I realised that in a way similar to how I removed my old coat to put on the new, we take off our old sinful nature to have it replaced with the nature of Christ.

I realised anew that because of Christ, I can go out into life's storms with confidence, just as I can go out into the winter weather, knowing that my new coat will keep me warm and protected from the weather.

Prayer: *God of mercy and grace, thank you for surprising us with your goodness. Thank you for the best gift of all, salvation given through your Son, Jesus Christ. Amen*

Thought for the day: Salvation is the best gift of all.

Rebecca Seaton (Tennessee, US)

When Things Go Wrong

Read Matthew 1:18–25
All things work together for good for those who love God.
Romans 8:28 (NRSV)

Sometimes life seems completely wrong. A situation we find ourselves in, the turn a job has taken, even relationships with people we thought we knew and loved go wrong. Why is this happening? What did we do to deserve this?

Joseph must have wondered the same thing. He has been awaiting his marriage to Mary, and now he finds himself betrayed by his fiancée. But Joseph is a man of grace and decides to divorce Mary quietly so she will not risk rejection from the community, or even worse. We do not know how long Joseph wrestles with this decision or how long he searches for the best way to handle the situation. Mary had probably thought that saying yes to God would be a blessing, and Joseph dreamed of a very different future. God's role in all this is revealed to Joseph through a heavenly messenger. How different the story might have been if Joseph had refused to hear the truth!

Romans 8:28 promises us that all things work for good for those who love God. Often it does not seem that way. Nursing an old injury may keep us from accepting the truth. This Advent season is the perfect time to release these old hurts and accept the gifts of love and grace, peace and mercy that await us when we receive the miracle of God's greatest gift.

Prayer: *Holy God, give us eyes to see and ears to hear so we may sense the work you are doing in our lives. Amen*

Thought for the day: When we let go of old hurts, we make more room for God's peace.

Susan Engle (Kentucky, US)

Like the Shepherds

Read Luke 2:8–15

The shepherds said one to another, Let us now go even unto Bethlehem, and see this thing which is come to pass, which the Lord hath made known unto us. And the shepherds returned, glorifying and praising God for all the things that they had heard and seen.
Luke 2:15, 20 (KJV)

Some of the Christmas story's significant people are anonymous. Consider the shepherds who were tending their sheep on the night Jesus was born. They unexpectedly became part of history's greatest event, the birth of God's Son. Even though the shepherds were unprepared, they became willing participants. After the angel announced the marvellous birth, the shepherds decided to go and see for themselves. At the manger, they revealed the good news the angel had proclaimed. Then, as they returned to their sheep, they glorified and praised God for all they had heard and seen.

The shepherds serve as models for people of faith today. God continues to come to us in unexpected ways and at unexpected times. Our most faithful response is to listen to and then to tell others what God asks of us. We can also emulate the shepherds by glorifying and praising God. Who knows? We might become anonymous but significant participants in history.

Prayer: *Dear Lord, help us to receive you when you come to us so we can tell of our experience and sing to your glory. Amen*

Thought for the day: How has God shown up unexpectedly in my life?

Wayne Smith (Georgia, US)

Gift Wrapped

Read Genesis 18:1–14

The Lord said to Abraham, 'Why did Sarah laugh…? Is anything too wonderful for the Lord?'
Genesis 18:13–14 (NRSV)

Gift giving is a major part of our celebration of the Christmas season. Gifts come in various forms: some in beautifully decorated packages, some in well-meaning words, others in kind deeds. Gifts symbolise the giver's love and appreciation for the receiver. Gifts can bring joy as well as wonder.

The gift Sarah received so surprised her that she laughed in disbelief. God gave her a gift in the news that she would become a mother. This gift fulfilled God's promise to her husband, Abraham, concerning his lineage. And many generations later, Abraham's descendants would receive the gift of God's Son, Jesus Christ, through a young woman named Mary. Like Sarah, Mary was surprised at her news from God. Sarah laughed, and Mary pondered (see Luke 1:26–29). Mary's gift was to be the mother of God's everlasting gift to the world.

During the Christmas season, we are reminded of God's gift to us: Emmanuel, which means 'God with us'. Jesus is a reminder of God's enduring love for us. We receive this gift with joy, knowing that God wrapped it with love and sealed it with grace.

Prayer: *Dear Giver of all that is good, what a joy it is to receive your love. Teach us to share it with others as a token of our gratitude to you. Amen*

Thought for the day: Christ is God's most wonderful gift to the world.

Carlene Lenore Douglas (Tennessee, US)

Clinging to Christ

Read Romans 8:35–39

Paul wrote, 'I am convinced that neither death nor life… neither the present nor the future… nor anything else in all creation, will be able to separate us from the love of God that is in Christ Jesus our Lord.'
Romans 8:38–39 (NIV)

I was not brought up in a church-going home. My real relationship in Christ began in 1972 when a few of my 'Jesus-freak' college friends gently persuaded me that Christ ought to take a central position in my life. Still, distractions cause me to struggle with living this precept. What sustains me is clinging to Christ through using resources like *The Upper Room*. Through what I read here, I have become convinced that our 'clinging' will bring us opportunities to serve and to feel the satisfaction of our relationship with Christ.

One such opportunity for me came in 1980 as I was bidding goodbye to my father, who was dying from Motor Neurone Disease. I wanted to offer him God's peace. I read to him Romans 8:35–39. Within a month he was gone, but before he died my mother wrote me a letter that brought me peace as well. She told me that Dad had been comforted by the words from Romans that I had read to him. He was also glad that I had come to know Christ on my own. But it wasn't really on my own; it was all because of the awareness and desire to cling to Christ, planted in me by the loving actions of others who cared for me.

Prayer: *Dear Father, show us how we can bring peace to others and find peace ourselves. In Jesus' name we pray. Amen*

Thought for the day: Clinging to Christ strengthens us to share Christ's love.

Mike Halpin (Texas, US)

My Gift

Read Exodus 33:12–17
He calls his own sheep by name.
John 10:3 (NIV)

One Christmas when my son, Steve, was about eight years old, he came home from Sunday school with a present from his teacher. 'I got a gift with my name on it,' he announced proudly. I was puzzled. I knew that all the children had received similar gifts. Why was it so important to him that the gift had his name on it? He explained that the teacher had chosen this particular version of the gift with him in mind. As he had looked around the room, he knew that she had chosen the gift that was the best one for him. He felt special.

God offers me gifts at Christmas: the gifts of redemption, forgiveness and a restored relationship with the creator through the Son, Jesus. God offers the same gift to everyone, but my salvation is unique to who I am. It is more than a generic gift with a tag that says, 'To: Anyone'. It has my name on it. My relationship with God is unique to who I am, with my personality, gifts and abilities. God sees me and each of us as an individual who is special and worth loving. What an amazing gift!

Prayer: *Thank you, God, for the gift of your love seen in Jesus Christ. Amen*

Thought for the day: God offers each of us a unique relationship of love.

Link2Life: *Give a gift to someone new this Christmas.*

Bernice Karnop (Montana, US)

Liberating Act

Read Luke 6:27–31

If anyone wants to sue you and take your coat, give your cloak as well; and if anyone forces you to go one mile, go also the second mile.
Matthew 5:40-41 (NRSV)

I spent two years buying furnishings for the home that would give me independence from my parents. God blessed me with a house for my husband, my child and me. We had been living there for only three weeks when my husband asked for a divorce. We hired a solicitor to help us divide our few belongings, which included a car that I used as a part of my work. I saw my meagre financial resources slipping through my fingers and my one major asset taken from me. I felt as if I were drowning.

I had to return to my parents' house. I was desperate when I arrived there. In agony, I picked up the Bible and randomly leafed through the pages. I read Matthew 5:41. Then, feeling that this was what God wanted me to do in the situation with my husband, I cried until I was exhausted.

The following day, instead of complaining about losing my possessions, I told my ex-husband, 'Take everything. It is my gift to you.' Detaching myself from my possessions liberated me from suffering and injustice. I felt at peace. A month after that episode, my ex-husband abandoned his desire for vengeance and returned everything I had given him.

I shall never forget what God did for me. Many years have passed, but I still live by this practice of detaching myself from possessions. It continues to set me free.

Prayer: *Merciful God, remain by our side, speaking to us and comforting us. Amen*

Thought for the day: When God speaks, listen.
Noris Jacqueline Cáceres (Espaillat, Dominican Republic)

The Holy Name

Read Matthew 6:9–13

Give ear to my words, O Lord, consider my sighing. Listen to my cry for help, my King and my God, for to you I pray.
Psalm 5:1–2 (NIV)

My six-year-old and I were saying the Lord's Prayer. Her careful articulation of the words and her sincerity struck me. I have recited the prayer for years, sometimes with little thought, but that night I saw its meaning in a new way.

Over Christmas, we will be moving to live in a different part of the country. You might think that 'Give us today our daily bread' would have spoken to me that night. But as we prayed 'Hallowed be your name' (Matthew 6:9), I knew that God wanted to be the Lord over all aspects of my life, not just my job or my home. My tendency to worry, my striving to make all things right, our plans for the move, the way we rear our children, my friendships, my care for those in need—all of these are God's.

Praying the Lord's Prayer made me realise that no matter how crazy our lives or circumstances seem, we can depend solely on God in everything—our joy and all our messy pain. As we move away from what has been home, remembering that we can depend on God is a comforting thought.

Prayer: *Thank you, Lord, for your boundless and unfathomable love. May we hallow your name in every area of our life. As Jesus taught us, we pray, 'Our Father in heaven, hallowed be your name, your kingdom come, your will be done on earth as it is in heaven. Give us today our daily bread. Forgive us our debts, as we also have forgiven our debtors. And lead us not into temptation, but deliver us from the evil one.'* Amen*

Thought for the day: Whatever burden we bear, God's shoulders are strong enough to carry it for us.

Katherine Reay (Texas, US)

PRAYER FOCUS: FAMILIES MOVING TO A NEW HOME

* Matthew 6:9–13 (NIV)

Universal News

Read Luke 1:26–33

The angel said to them, 'Do not be afraid. I bring you good news of great joy that will be for all the people.'
Luke 2:10 (NIV)

While working a crossword puzzle from the newspaper, I saw that many answers were Christmas greetings heard in cities around the world. I knew the holiday wishes for Manchester (Merry Christmas) and Madrid (Feliz Navidad), but I had to look up the greetings for Oslo (Gledelig Jul), Oahu (Mele Kalikimaka), Paris (Joyeux Noël), Rome (Buon Natale), and Seoul (Chook Sung Tan).

The very first Christmas greeting came from an angel: 'Do not be afraid. I bring you good news of great joy that will be for all the people. Today in the town of David a Saviour has been born to you; he is Christ the Lord' (Luke 2:10–11). The angel shared this news with some shepherds. Initially these night-shift workers were terrified but eventually calmed down. They went to Bethlehem, found the baby and his parents, and went back to work 'glorifying and praising God' (Luke 2:20).

As the holiday greetings in the crossword puzzle show, the angel's message has gone around the world. We join with countless believers throughout the world in rejoicing, as did the shepherds, over the good news of God's coming to us.

Prayer: *O God, help us to join the angels and other believers in proclaiming to the world the good news of your love. Amen*

Thought for the day: The good news of Christ's birth is the greatest news the world has ever received.

Greg Garland (Virginia, US)

Sweet Treasures

Read Deuteronomy 11:13–21

Fix these words of mine in your hearts and minds; tie them as symbols on your hands and bind them on your foreheads. Teach them to your children, talking about them when you sit at home and when you walk along the road, when you lie down and when you get up.
Deuteronomy 11:18–19 (NIV)

When I was a child, my Sunday school teacher gave us stickers for every achievement and sweets to everyone who memorised a Bible verse correctly. I began to memorise as many verses as I could each week so I could get extra sweets. I ended up knowing hundreds of verses!

During my teenage years, I became a youth leader in a rural area. Most of the young people there didn't own a Bible, and my knowledge of Bible verses became a big asset to my work.

Now when I look back on those times, I thank God for my Sunday school teacher who encouraged us to learn the Bible. While my memorising Bible verses began only because I loved sweets, that habit matured into meaningful study of the scriptures, so that from the age of 16, I have been able to enrich my life and the lives of others. Now, as a parent, I share my experiences with my children and encourage them in our daily prayer time to learn—yes, even memorise—God's word.

Prayer: *Thank you, Lord, for those who teach children your word. Give us eagerness and willingness to be part of your work. In Jesus' name. Amen*

Thought for the day: Meditating on Bible verses is the beginning of applying them to our life.

Charlotte Mande Ilunga (Cape Town, South Africa)

The Word Becomes Flesh

Read John 1:9–14

Blessed be the God… of all consolation, who consoles us in all our affliction, so that we may be able to console those who are in any affliction with the consolation with which we ourselves are consoled by God.

2 Corinthians 1:3–4 (NRSV)

A few days before Christmas, I had an emotional visit with the family of a patient who was near death. Afterwards, though my chaplain shift was over, for some reason I decided to walk back through the emergency unit. I noticed Jennie sitting on her bed, crying, in great pain. She was in her 20s, and after years of alcohol abuse she had taken her last drink the day before. She had given up. 'I have ruined my life; my family hates me; I have no reason to live. Oh God!' she said.

I held Jennie's hand and said to her, 'Your decision to quit was very difficult and courageous. God loves you and sees you as a person of high value, with unique and special gifts.' I continued, 'I struggled with alcohol, too. I have sat where you sit now. Years from now, you will be able to assure someone else, "With God's help, you can get through this pain. I did."' Peace soon came over Jennie's face, and she lay down to rest.

Through the Holy Spirit, God became flesh at Christmas. And God becomes flesh again in us whenever we share with others the comfort we have received from our creator.

Prayer: *O God, help us be Christ in the flesh for someone in a time of need. In Jesus' name we pray. Amen*

Thought for the day: Sometimes the word goes forth through a gentle touch and word of encouragement.

Dan Nelson (North Carolina, US)

When All Seems Lost

Read 1 John 1:1–7

Jesus spoke to them, saying, 'I am the light of the world. Whoever follows me will never walk in darkness but will have the light of life.'
John 8:12 (NRSV)

For years my husband and I have celebrated Advent by lighting the candles of an Advent wreath and using the litanies that appear in *The Upper Room* magazine. Each Sunday, we wait for our sons and our grandchildren to arrive so we can include them in our worship time. Our grandchildren delight in lighting the candles. The questions in the litany cause us to pause and reflect. And as we talk, we learn more about one another and our faith.

This year, early on Christmas Eve we lit the four Advent candles of hope, peace, joy and love. Then, after lighting the Christ candle, we left them burning. That evening, I found my eyes continually drawn to the wreath while our home filled with laughter and music, excited children, and adults telling old memories and stories.

Late into the night, I was seated nearby, watching as the candles began to burn out. The candle of hope burned out first, followed by the candles of peace, joy and love. Yet the Christ candle burned on. And I realised once again that when all seems lost, I need only Christ to show me the way.

Prayer: *Dear God, when hope, peace, joy or love seem lost, remind us that Christ is always with us to light our way. Amen*

Thought for the day: Christ is always with me.

Leslie Coleman (Florida, US)

PRAYER FOCUS: THOSE FEELING OVERWHELMED BY LIFE

Christmas Awe

Read John 1:35–41

An angel of the Lord appeared to them, and the glory of the Lord shone around them, and they were terrified… When they had seen [the baby], they spread the word concerning what had been told them about this child.

Luke 2:9, 17 (NIV)

As my wife and I walked from the church gate holding hands with our four-year-old son, a heavily bearded man approached us from the opposite direction. I had seen the man before and was familiar with his fast-paced gait but had not noticed him more than to exchange occasional greetings.

Upon seeing the man, my son shouted, 'Daddy, see Jesus coming right in front of us!' We broke out in laughter. Apparently, my son's image of Jesus came from the children's Bible story books and films that depict Jesus as a heavily bearded, light-skinned man. As I chuckled, I remembered the shepherds who were watching over their flocks on the night Christ was born. I imagined how startled and frightened they must have been. Reflecting on this, I admired my son's courage and excitement at seeing and meeting 'Jesus' that day.

As we celebrate Christmas, my son's exclamation reminds me to look for Jesus. When we focus on Christ instead of being distracted by the many interruptions we encounter every day, we are able to spread the word about his birth and saving grace for all people!

Prayer: *God of all seasons, as we commemorate your Son's birth give us childlike awe and enthusiasm for spreading his message of hope. Amen*

Thought for the day: How am I looking for Jesus this Christmas season?

Philip Polo (Nairobi Area, Kenya)

The Right Investment

Read Matthew 6:19–21

Store up for yourselves treasures in heaven.
Matthew 6:20 (NIV)

For some time now I have been helping an extremely poor family—a mother with three children—to survive. Sometimes I give them money; at other times I take them clothes or other items they need. One day, the mother asked me for some more money. I told her I was not able to offer her any just then. A few days later I bought a tool that I had needed for a long time. At first I was excited about my purchase, but soon I thought of that mother and her children. The money I had spent for the tool could have bought their food for several days.

As I continued to think about what I had done, I found myself in a dilemma. On one hand, I blamed myself for not having given the mother money. On the other hand, I excused myself by saying, 'I need this tool; it's an investment to help me earn even more money to help even more people.' That sounded good, but I had no peace in my heart. The tool wasn't the right investment. The tool was something that would, in time, rust and become useless. But Jesus told us that the treasures we store up in heaven will never rust; they will last for ever.

I vowed to be careful about my investments—about where I use my material and spiritual resources.

Prayer: *Dear God, help us to make good investments—ones that will bring hope and healing to your people. Amen*

Thought for the day: How can I use my resources to help those in need?

George Enchev (Bulgaria)

The Evergreen Word

Read 1 Peter 1:23–25

All flesh is like grass and all its glory like the flower of grass. The grass withers, and the flower falls, but the word of the Lord endures forever.
1 Peter 1:24–25 (NRSV)

Every spring my husband and I plant colourful flowers in four large pots, and my husband dutifully tends to the lawn by reseeding, watering and fertilising. At first we can barely see the plants above the rims of the pots, but in a few weeks they begin to rise from the soil as if some magnet were pulling them upward. The grass turns a lush green, bringing the weekly chore of mowing. Every morning we have coffee on our patio. My eyes never tire of the luminous array of colours. Then, as if someone pulled the plug, the beautiful flowers begin to fade. The blooms fall off, leaving only ugly stems. The once-luxurious green lawn turns a dingy brown, and seemingly overnight, all the colours are gone. Winter has arrived.

Almost everything wears out, grows old or fades. However, one thing that is always new and reliable is the word of God. For thousands of years, the Bible has continued to offer the message of salvation, bring comfort to the weary and show us the right path to walk. It never withers, fades or grows obsolete. It remains as fresh and lovely as those first blooms of spring.

Prayer: *Let your message, O Lord, light our path. Amen*

Thought for the day: Knowing more of the Bible means knowing more of God.

Mary Baird (Texas, US)

Shine!

Read Ephesians 1:11–14

In [Christ] you also, when you had heard the word of truth, the gospel of your salvation, and had believed in him, were marked with the seal of the promised Holy Spirit.
Ephesians 1:13 (NSRV)

My son has some light reflectors fastened to his school bag. The reason for the reflectors is not fashion but safety. When a car's headlights shine on the bag, the reflectors tell the driver that a pedestrian is ahead. In every school there are posters that advertise this safety practice: 'Be noticed'; 'Shine, so you can be safe'.

Seeing these reflectors reminded me of when I repented of my sins more than ten years ago. The Holy Spirit marked me with a seal, and in the light of God's divine love I began to shine. I am an ordinary person, but when I reflect God's divine light I can shine even in the bustle of everyday life. Reflecting God's light can disperse the darkness around me. When faced with despair, I can be joyful. When anxiety surrounds me, I can be calm. Where there is evil, I can embody love. Where there is indifference, I can be engaged.

All this is possible when we are in Christ and he lives in us. Jesus said in Matthew 5:14, 'You are the light of the world.' Let us reflect Christ's light every day!

Prayer: *O God, help us to realise that when we walk in your light we can reflect your love to those around us. Amen*

Thought for the day: How am I reflecting God's light to those near me?

Natalya Ilyushonok (Hrodna, Belarus)

A Stranger's Prayer

Read Romans 8:22–30

The Spirit helps us in our weakness. We do not know what we ought to pray for, but the Spirit… intercedes for us with groans that words cannot express.
Romans 8:26 (NIV)

In the days before my mother's bypass surgery, she asked me many times to pray for her. I prayed silent prayers asking God to heal her, but I could never pray aloud as I knew she wanted me to.

The day came for Mum's surgery. As the hospital worker began pushing my mother's bed out of the hospital ward door, Mum asked the woman to pray for her. The hospital worker stopped pushing the bed, shut the door and immediately began praying for my mother. Her prayer was powerful and dynamic.

God wants us to pray for one another. Our prayers can be silent or spoken. They can be eloquent or simple. We speak from our hearts to God, who hears even the silent cries of our soul.

Prayer: *Dear God, we don't always know the right words to pray for those who are sick and afraid. Give us the courage and, when they are needed, the words to pray for those who need your healing grace. Amen*

Thought for the day: To pray for another is a gift of love.

Jennifer Woods (Arkansas, US)

A Season for Everything

Read Ecclesiastes 3:1–8

For everything there is a season, and a time for every matter under heaven.
Ecclesiastes 3:1 (NRSV)

On my morning walks I often pass an urban community garden. City residents have divided empty ground into small, garden-sized plots. Once these gardens were filled with flowers and vegetables. But recently I walked by and saw no flowers, no colour, seemingly no fruit. Why? We had early snow and ice last week. It's the season when in our part of the world gardens lie fallow. But come spring, avid gardeners will once again see fruit in their garden plots.

Like that garden, we have seasons of colour and obvious fruitfulness and fallow times when we don't grow as much. Sometimes a fallow time comes after an icy experience. Maybe we've suffered adversity or a loss. Maybe we don't feel useful anymore. The wise writer of Ecclesiastes tells us that 'every matter under heaven' has its season. Some of these are not happy times. For example, there is 'a time to mourn... a time to keep silence' (Ecclesiastes 3:4, 7). That sounds like a fallow season when we aren't colourful and growing. But because we know God, we live in trust that springtime and fruitfulness will come again.

Prayer: *Good and gracious God, help us to hope and trust in your ongoing work in our lives. Amen*

Thought for the day: God is at work for good even in our fallow seasons.

Mark Abbott (Washington, US)

Set Free

Read Luke 4:16–21

Then Jesus said to the Jews who had believed in him, 'If you continue in my word, you are truly my disciples; and you will know the truth, and the truth will make you free.'
John 8:31–32 (NRSV)

A few minutes' walk from my home is our county's main prison. The walls are high and solid. I cannot see into the prison, nor can the inmates see beyond the walls. The inmates have cells, beds with linen, reasonable meals and a roof over their heads. But what none of them has is freedom. They cannot do what they like or go where they like, when they like. They do as they're told. For some, this captivity will go on for years.

Jesus, who said he was truth, also said, 'The truth will make you free.' Part of Jesus' mission was to proclaim release to the captives (see Luke 4:18), but he meant more than those forcibly kept in prisons. He surely was referring to those of us who are captive to addictions or to bitterness coming from a hurt we suffered years ago or perhaps to damaging relationships within family, marriage or between friends.

If we're in captivity to those things or anything else, it doesn't have to go on. Christ wants to set us free—starting today.

Prayer: *Thank you, O God, that when we know you we can live free. Give us the courage to do what we need to do to experience the freedom you offer. In Jesus' name we pray. Amen*

Thought for the day: Christ offers us release from whatever imprisons us.

Richard William Lawton (South Australia, Australia)

Small Group Questions

Wednesday 5 September

1. When have you been part of fundraising to help a friend, colleague or church member with medical bills? How did you feel about doing this? If you've not done it, what holds you back from participating?

2. How does your church help those who cannot pay their medical bills? How do you preserve the dignity of those you help?

3. Where is free or reduced-cost medical care available in your community? If you don't know, what would be good about finding this out, and how might you use the information? How does your church support community health initiatives?

4. One translation of Titus 3:14 tells believers to meet 'real needs' as an expression of faith. What real needs have you personally helped to meet recently? What real needs has your church met?

5. What's the difference between random acts of kindness and Christian compassion? Or is there no difference? Why do you answer as you do?

6. How do you fit helping others into your daily life? Why is it important for believers to make helping others a regular part of their life?

Wednesday 12 September

1. How do you respond to scripture's admonition to pray without ceasing? Is this really possible, or do you think the admonition is meant only as an ideal?

2. Where do your ideas about how much we 'should' pray come from? How have your ideas about this changed over time?

3. What activities or places often turn your thoughts to God? How could you build on this to strengthen your prayer?

4. When you need prayer, whom do you ask to pray for you, and why?

5. Do you talk to God as you would to a friend, or do you use more formal language when you pray than you do in everyday conversation? What are the advantages and effects of each of these ways of addressing God?

6. When have you heard God speak to you through the words of a friend or fellow believer? What makes you say this was God speaking?

7. How will your prayers be different in the coming week because of your group's conversation about this meditation?

Wednesday 19 September

1. Did you come to personal faith early or late in your life? What is good about your way of coming to know God?

2. What do you think Valdeko means by 'God heard my knock and opened the door'? If you knew Valdeko when this happened, what might you have seen to indicate that God was at work in his life?

3. Valdeko's faith causes him to see 'that nature is wonderful and people can be amiable'. Is this true for you? What do you appreciate more deeply than you used to because of your faith?

4. How has your spiritual life changed as you have grown older? Do you see the changes as good or bad, and why?

5. Do you know anyone who has gone to theological college in middle or late adulthood? If so, what helped them to do so?

6. How might we all come to Valdeko's exuberance about our faith? When was the last time you felt energised and positive about serving God? Is it possible to sustain such a feeling? Why do you say this?

Wednesday 26 September

1. Do you identify with this young mother's struggle to get to church? What challenges do you face in getting to church regularly?

2. How do you 'keep the sabbath'? What is a true sabbath for you, offering physical renewal and closeness to God?

3. What is your ministry? How have you come to know this? If you haven't identified it, would you like the group to help you do so?

4. Whom do you call when you feel as Renee's friend did—overwhelmed or lonely? Why this person or these persons?

5. Who do you know who seems lonely? How can you reach out to that person to show the love of God? When will you take the first step to do that?

6. What ordinary activities can you see as ministry to others? When has some 'non-religious' action been an expression of God's love and care to you?

Wednesday 3 October

1. Are you like Joanna, unable to point to a particular moment when you 'became a Christian'? If so, how would you respond to someone asking how you can be sure that you are? If you can point to a moment you began a conscious walk with Christ, how does your level of assurance compare with Joanna's witness?

2. Many people seem to worry about whether they are 'really a Christian' or are 'really saved'. What causes this fear/worry? Do you ever experience it? If so, what helps you at such times?

3. How would you respond to someone who says they aren't sure whether they are in right relationship with God but want to be?

4. Compare Paul's conversion experience on the road to Damascus (Acts 9:1–19) with the Emmaus travellers' experience in coming to recognise Jesus (Luke 24:13–33). What do the stories have in common? How do they differ? Which one gets more attention in church?

5. What is the outward evidence that you are a Christian? Do your neighbours know that you are Christian? Should all Christians' neighbours know that we are believers? Is it possible truly to be a Christian and not have anyone know it?

6. What scripture verses assure you that you are a Christian?

Wednesday 10 October

1. Read aloud Matthew 13:18–23. What can we do to prepare our spirit to be 'good soil' for what God wants to grow in us?

2. What lessons has God taught you through the natural world?

3. How is comparing our Christian growth to the growth of a plant helpful and instructive? Where does the comparison fail or become inaccurate?

4. How does your faith community plant seed inside the community of faith? How does it plant seed outside? What fruit have you seen come from these efforts?

5. What way/ways of studying the Bible has/have been most effective for you? Name one or two ways your behaviour has changed because of studying the Bible.

6. How have you experienced God nurturing you in the past week? Had you identified this as God's activity before you heard/read this question? If so, how did you realise this?

Wednesday 17 October

1. What scene or experience came to mind when you read the opening paragraph of this meditation? Were you an actor in the scene you remembered or an observer? Why do you remember it?

2. If you were the next customer in line and had observed Gale's rudeness, what might you have done to show compassion and empathy to the assistant? Have you ever actually done this after seeing someone mistreated? When would it be appropriate to say or do something, and when not?

3. Have you ever done something like Gale did, publicly mistreating someone? Did you apologise? Why or why not?

4. Gale expresses thanks for God's loving him enough to correct him. How might we remember to think of a sense of wrongdoing in this way in the future?

5. How could the assistant have responded to Gale as a Christian witness to him and other customers? How could you adapt that answer for use at times when you are mistreated?

6. What Bible verses come to mind as you consider this meditation?

Wednesday 24 October

1. How does your faith community finance mission trips and mission outreach?

2. Who in your faith community has a talent for cooking or some other 'ordinary' gift that benefits all of you? How can we recognise and publicly affirm such gifts?

3. Why do many people think, feel and say that they have no special gifts or talents? How can we, within communities of faith, help people to identify their gifts and use them for God's purposes outside the church's walls?

4. Who do you know who has a gift of hospitality? What makes you say this?

5. How do you support your church's mission outreaches in your community and in the wider world? Where would you like to do more? What ideas for doing so can you pull from today's meditation?

6. How could the members of this discussion group engage in mission together? Why will you do so, or why not?

Wednesday 31 October

1. What is your earliest memory of contact with someone of a different race? What feelings or attitudes are attached to the memory?

2. Do you agree or disagree with this parent's explanation of racial differences? How is it helpful? Was it appropriate for a child? Is it appropriate for adults?

3. What experiences have you had with people from other countries and cultures? What have you learned from them? How do you see the world differently because of these experiences?

4. In what sense are we all God's children?

5. How and why should Christians work for racial inclusiveness and economic and social justice?

6. What Bible passages lead you to believe that God wills that all people of all races and cultures be clothed, fed, and equally loved and respected?

Wednesday 7 November

1. What's the worst losing-a-job story you've heard? What made the situation so hard?

2. What do you think people mean when they say 'God never closes a door without opening a window'? From your own life, would you say this is true or not, and why?

3. How can we 'change thoughts of fear into anticipation'? Is doing so difficult or easy?

4. How might a situation like the one Noel faced invite us to become more like Christ? Where would you like to become more like Christ?

5. Noel says that our perception of a situation can affect our sense of peace. How is this true? What are the limits of saying so?

6. How can we open ourselves to God's peace when life seems chaotic?

Wednesday 14 November

1. How often and in what ways were you interrupted today? Looking back, how might these interruptions have been opportunities to serve God and others?

2. What's the difference between focusing on what we need to do and shutting ourselves off from others and their needs? How can we balance the two?

3. When for you has an ordinary interaction with someone led to a discovery of sadness, need or fear? How did you respond? Were you aware of the interaction as a way to serve God?

4. Read Matthew 9:18–32. How many times is Jesus interrupted in this passage? How does he respond? What is Jesus' concern and attitude in these stories? What lessons can we draw from this for dealing with our interruptions?

5. What most often keeps you from listening to others? How does listening compassionately move beyond politeness to become a Christian act?

6. What can we do to prepare ourselves to pay attention to God's call coming through interruptions or daily annoyances?

Wednesday 21 November

1. What is the first Bible verse you became familiar with, and where/how did you encounter it? Did you or did you not memorise it, and why?

2. What was your favourite, special treat-to-eat when you were a child, and who provided it? How was it important as more than food? What's your favourite food treat now, and why?

3. How has friendship with other believers helped you want to know and get to know the Bible better? How would your friends answer this question about you?

4. Which Christian (living or dead) has most shaped you to become more like Christ? How did this come about?

5. When was the last time you received a handwritten note or letter, and from whom? When was the last time you wrote one? When and why do you write messages by hand when you could use another means?

6. How can we keep interactions personal when handwritten messages are being displaced by electronic ones? How can/does electronic communication help us build relationships in ways we could not in the past?

Wednesday 28 November

1. What do people mean when they say they 'feel God's presence'? Are you a person who says that? If so, when and why did you last say it?

2. Why is it important for parents to pray with their children? Did your parents pray with you? If not, how and when did you learn to pray?

3. How does your church help single parents? Where and how would you like to see your congregation do a better job in supporting single parents?

4. What could a church do to help members who have lost their jobs? Is your church doing those things?

5. Why do you suppose the writer's 13-year-old son thought 'Help!' was a good prayer? Do you think it is? Why or why not?

6. The writer says that God 'lifted each burden from [her] heart' when she prayed, 'Help!' What do you think she means by this? What outward signs of change might cause us to say that someone's burden had been lifted?

7. What helps you to reconnect with God?

Wednesday 5 December

1. Do you agree that forgiving is hard? In what situations do you find it hard to forgive?

2. How is or should forgiveness be part of our ordinary days? When and where do we need to be ready to offer 'ordinary forgiveness'?

3. How would your day today have been different if you had been more forgiving? How could tomorrow be different if you forgave?

4. What's the difference between holding others accountable and judging them? How can we hold others accountable without seeming self-righteous?

5. Who has the right and privilege to hold us accountable for how we live our faith? In what kinds of relationships is this possible, and why? Do you have such relationships at the moment? How might this group be such a place? What would you have to do differently to make it so?

6. What is the most amazing example of forgiveness you've heard of? Could you have forgiven in the same way, for a similar action?

Wednesday 12 December

1. When does praying seem easy and natural for you? Are there particular situations or settings that often move you to pray?

2. Do you agree that there is always something to be thankful about? What are the top three things that you are thankful for today?

3. Today's quoted verse singles out the prayers of 'a good person'. Does God hear the prayers of some people more readily than others? Why do you say this?

4. What form of prayer—praise, confession, intercession, silent awe or some other—do you pray most often? Why so?

5. When was the last time you saw an unmistakable answer to prayer? Who prayed, and how did the answer come?

6. How has someone been an answer to your prayers recently?

7. When is praying not enough? In what circumstances should we 'put legs on our prayers' and act? How do we decide when to act as well as ask?

Wednesday 19 December

1. Do you have possessions, or do your possessions have you? What makes you say this?

2. When have you saved for something important to you or another person? How does it feel to reach a savings goal?

3. Whom do you know who has adult children living at home? What are the special challenges of such arrangements?

4. Do you think Noris should have given in to her husband? Why or why not?

5. How has divorce touched your family? What is your church doing to help those who are wounded by the end of a marriage?

6. What do you think Noris means by saying that she detaches herself from possessions? Why would she need to do it more than once?

7. Where in your life do you have 'abundance'? How do you use your abundance to serve God? How could you?

Wednesday 26 December

1. When was the last time you helped someone in need? How did you learn of the need, and what did you do to help?

2. Do you think George was justified in feeling guilty for buying the tool he mentioned? Why or why not? Was he too hard on himself?

3. How do you cope with the fact that you cannot help every needy person you see or know about? Do you think God expects you to help every one of them? If so, how? If not, how do you decide when to help and when not to?

4. Is guilt ever a good reason to give to another person? Why or why not?

5. How have you invested yourself in earthly treasures in the past week? How have you invested in heavenly treasures during that time?

6. When you are forced to choose between two good things, as George was (helping the family or buying a tool he needed), what helps you to decide?

Journal page

Journal page

Companions on the Bethlehem Road

Daily readings and reflections for the Advent journey

Rachel Boulding

This book of daily Bible readings and reflections for Advent and Christmas is based around spiritual insights gleaned from some of the best-loved poets of the past—Eliot, Herbert, Tennyson and Auden, among others. While they come from different ages and backgrounds, they wrestled with the same questions that we do, about God, love, hope and suffering.

There are so many aspects of God's love for us and ours for him that are hard to grasp. While we can glimpse only part of the picture, it often seems that, in poetry, our deepest yearnings can come to the surface. As we travel the road to Christmas in the company of these great poets, we will find our minds enlarged and our hearts touched with something of the wonder and joy of this special season.

Companions on the Bethlehem Road also includes a section of material for group discussion over five sessions.

ISBN 978 0 85746 065 3   £7.99
To order a copy of this book, please turn to the order form on page 159.

Paul as Pastor

Biblical insights for pastoral ministry

Patrick Whitworth

When we think of the apostle Paul, 'pastor' is not usually the first word that springs to mind. He may seem too intellectual, too tempestuous and fiery, even too determinedly pioneering, to fall into the 'pastoral' category. This book demonstrates that, at heart, Paul was indeed too multi-faceted in both background and ministry to be defined by a single function. He was an apostle, prophet, evangelist and teacher—but he was also a pastor, as we can see from reading the epistles that record his teaching and care of the churches he planted or nurtured.

Author Patrick Whitworth makes the case that Paul's extraordinary teaching—for which he is justifiably most celebrated—was a product of his pastoral care, which was itself a product of his pioneering and prophetic evangelism. Perhaps he was an unlikely pastor but he was, above all, passionate, and an inspiration to pastors everywhere, to be studied and emulated, fathomed and then followed.

The book includes a study guide with a wealth of questions for group discussion linked to each chapter.

ISBN 978 0 85746 046 2   £8.99
To order a copy of this book, please turn to the order form on page 159.

The Recovery of Love

Walking the way of wholeness

Naomi Starkey

'… *Washed flat and almost clean by the ebb of the tide, the sand is bare except for a single set of footprints. And—why are we not surprised?—there he is again, ahead of us, waiting. Although it is barely dawn, there is light enough to see his face, recognise his smile. The shadows have gone, for this in-between time, anyway. When he speaks, we know his voice, although we cannot place his accent. Five words; a question: "What do you really want?"'*

Some people like to be taken on mystery tours; others prefer to have a clear idea of where they are going, how long it will take, and where they will stop for lunch. This book is, in some ways, a bit of a mystery tour, exploring aspects of faith and truth through storytelling, reflection on Bible passages and quotations from other writers. At the heart of the narrative is the meaning of love: on the one hand, our hunger for it and often weary search to find it, and, on the other hand, God's breathtaking love for us.

ISBN 978 1 84101 892 8   £6.99
To order a copy of this book, please turn to the order form on page 159.

Bible Word Sudoku

Andrew Briggs

Do you like Sudoku? Or perhaps you think you might but you've never given it a try. Or perhaps somebody has given you this book as a present and you've no idea what to expect! Don't worry—these 80 Bible-based Sudoku puzzles are pitched at a relatively mild level and come complete with a helpful introduction on how to do Sudoku (as well as solutions at the back of the book...).

Doing puzzles like this is a good, fun way of expanding your knowledge of the Bible, its characters and its teachings. Some of the words hidden in these Sudoku problems will be familiar but others will not. As well as helping to solve the puzzle, looking up the references and reading about the words in context may well be helpful and encouraging to you personally.

ISBN 978 0 85746 058 5 £6.99
To order a copy of this book, please turn to the order form on page 159.

Bible Reading Resources Pack

Thank you for reading BRF Bible reading notes. BRF has been producing a variety of Bible reading notes for over 90 years, helping people all over the UK and the world connect with the Bible on a personal level every day.

Could you help us find other people who would enjoy our notes?

We produce a Bible Reading Resource Pack for church groups to use to encourage regular Bible reading.

This FREE pack contains:

- Samples of all BRF Bible reading notes.
- Our Resources for Personal Bible Reading catalogue, providing all you need to know about our Bible reading notes.
- A ready-to-use church magazine feature about BRF notes.
- Ready-made sermon and all-age service ideas to help your church into the Bible (ideal for Bible Sunday events).
- And much more!

How to order your FREE pack:

- Visit: www.biblereadingnotes.org.uk/request-a-bible-reading-resources-pack/
- Telephone: 01865 319700
- Post: Complete the form below and post to: Bible Reading Resource Pack, BRF, 15 The Chambers, Vineyard, Abingdon, OX14 3FE

Name..

Address ....

....Postcode..

Telephone ....

Email...

Please send me...................................Bible Reading Resources Pack(s).

This pack is produced free of charge for all UK addresses but, if you wish to offer a donation towards our costs, this would be appreciated. If you require a pack to be sent outside of the UK, please contact us for details of postage and packing charges. Tel: +44 1865 319700. Thank you.

Subscriptions

The Upper Room is published in January, May and September.

Individual subscriptions

The subscription rate for orders for 4 or fewer copies includes postage and packing: THE UPPER ROOM annual individual subscription £14.10

Church subscriptions

Orders for 5 copies or more, sent to ONE address, are post free:
THE UPPER ROOM annual church subscription £11.10

Please do not send payment with order for a church subscription. We will send an invoice with your first order.

Please note that the annual billing period for church subscriptions runs from 1 May to 30 April.

Copies of the notes may also be obtained from Christian bookshops.

Single copies of *The Upper Room* will cost £3.70. Prices valid until 30 April 2013.

Individual Subscriptions

☐ I would like to take out a subscription myself (complete your name and address details only once)

☐ I would like to give a gift subscription (please complete both name and address sections below)

Your name..

Your address..

....Postcode....................................

Your telephone number...

Gift subscription name...

Gift subscription address...

....Postcode....................................

Gift message (20 words max)..

....

Please send *The Upper Room* beginning with the January 2013 / May 2013 / September 2013 issue: (delete as applicable)

THE UPPER ROOM ☐ £14.10

Please complete the payment details below and send, with appropriate payment, to: BRF, 15 The Chambers, Vineyard, Abingdon OX14 3FE

Total enclosed £.......... (cheques should be made payable to 'BRF')

Payment by ☐ cheque ☐ postal order ☐ Visa ☐ Mastercard ☐ Switch

Card no: ⬚⬚⬚⬚⬚⬚⬚⬚⬚⬚⬚⬚⬚⬚⬚⬚⬚⬚⬚⬚

Expires: ⬚⬚⬚⬚ Security code: ⬚⬚⬚

Issue no (Switch): ⬚⬚⬚⬚

Signature (essential if paying by credit/Switch card) ....

☐ Please do not send me further information about BRF publications

☐ Please send me a Bible reading resources pack to encourage Bible reading in my church

BRF is a Registered Charity

Church Subscriptions

☐ Please send me ... copies of *The Upper Room* January 2013 / May 2013 / September 2013 issue (delete as applicable)

Name...

Address ....

....Postcode..

Telephone ....

Email...

Please send this completed form to:
BRF, 15 The Chambers, Vineyard, Abingdon OX14 3FE

Please do not send payment with this order. We will send an invoice with your first order.

Christian bookshops: All good Christian bookshops stock BRF publications. For your nearest stockist, please contact BRF.

Telephone: The BRF office is open between 09.15 and 17.30. To place your order, telephone 01865 319700; fax 01865 319701.

Web: Visit www.brf.org.uk

☐ Please send me a Bible reading resources pack to encourage Bible reading in my church

BRF is a Registered Charity

ORDERFORM

REF	TITLE	PRICE	QTY	TOTAL
065 3	Companions on the Bethlehem Road	£7.99		
046 2	Paul as Pastor	£8.99		
892 8	The Recovery of Love	£6.99		
058 5	Bible Word Sudoku	£6.99		

POSTAGE AND PACKING CHARGES				
Order value	UK	Europe	Surface	Air Mail
£7.00 & under	£1.25	£3.00	£3.50	£5.50
£7.01–£30.00	£2.25	£5.50	£6.50	£10.00
Over £30.00	FREE	prices on request		

Postage and packing	
Donation	
TOTAL	

Name _____ Account Number _____

Address _____

_____ Postcode _____

Telephone Number_____

Email _____

Payment by: ❏ Cheque ❏ Mastercard ❏ Visa ❏ Postal Order ❏ Maestro

Card no ▢▢▢▢ ▢▢▢▢ ▢▢▢▢ ▢▢▢▢ ▢▢▢

Valid from ▢▢▢▢   Expires ▢▢▢▢   Issue no. ▢▢▢

Security code* ▢▢▢   *Last 3 digits on the reverse of the card.   Shaded boxes for
                       ESSENTIAL IN ORDER TO PROCESS YOUR ORDER   Maestro use only

Signature _____ Date _____

All orders must be accompanied by the appropriate payment.

Please send your completed order form to:
BRF, 15 The Chambers, Vineyard, Abingdon OX14 3FE
Tel. 01865 319700 / Fax. 01865 319701 Email: enquiries@brf.org.uk

❏ Please send me further information about BRF publications.

Available from your local Christian bookshop.   BRF is a Registered Charity